GALIT SHMUELI

CW00838785

PRACTICAL RISK ANALYSIS FOR PROJECT PLANNING

A HANDS-ON GUIDE USING EXCEL®

WITH DATA AND EXAMPLES FROM BHUTAN

Copyright © 2011 Galit Shmueli

ISBN-13: 978-1-466-43064-8

ISBN-10: 1-466-43064-8

Cover art: Wangdue Phodrang Dzong, Bhutan. Copyright © 2011 Galit Shmueli

ALL RIGHTS RESERVED. Printed in the United States of America. No part of this work may be used or reproduced, transmitted, stored or used in any form or by any means graphic, electronic, or mechanical, including but not limited to photocopying, recording, scanning, digitizing, taping, Web distribution, information networks or information storage and retrieval systems, or in any manner whatsoever without prior written permission.

For further information see www.galitshmueli.com

First Edition, October 2011

Contents

4

Dedicated to those in search of a practical guide to handling uncertainty, evaluating risk, and integrating data into their decisions

Preface

THIS BOOK AROSE FROM A WORKSHOP THAT I DESIGNED IN 2008, during a sabbatical from the University of Maryland spent at the Rigsum Institute of Information Technology and Management in Thimphu, the capital of Bhutan. After spending a few months in Bhutan and studying local decision making practices, I noticed a critical need for data-driven planning. From conversations with business people in the private sector, with managers in the corporate world and government officials, I learned that many project decisions are made on a hunch. While this is the case in almost every country, in Bhutan it is more visible due to the close-knit, small population and the honest and outgoing nature of the locals, at all levels of society.

Unlike my students at the University of Maryland who were at the MBA or PhD levels, the workshop was intended for anyone at a managerial position with knowledge of basic Excel. Given this need and the intended audience, I designed a three-day "crash", hands-on workshop called "Decision Making Using Excel". The workshop focused on integrating data into the decision making process at the project planning stage and at the post-execution stage. I used local examples and local data to make the material closer to home, but the principles and methods are part of the general scientific toolkit for addressing uncertainty and risk. The workshop was offered multiple times during my year-long sabbatical. In 2010 I returned to the Rigsum Institute, re-introducing the workshop. I have since further refined the workshop and upgraded the Excel routines to Excel 2007 and 2010. The book is a product of the workshop, and based on what I learned from catering to a wide audience: from small entrepreneurs to high-level management; from government agencies to corporate and international organizations to the private sector; and from a wide spectrum of industries, including telecom, financial services, tourism, construction, energy (power and hydropower), agriculture, health, retail and education.

This book concentrates on the stage of *project planning*, when decisions need to be made on whether to invest in or implement a project, or how to choose among a set of projects. The main focus is on methods for assessing performance and risk of projects of interest under different scenarios and uncertainty, when they are still at the planning stage. Unlike many project planning books, this book focuses on integrating numerical data, combined with domain knowledge, into simple spreadsheet software such as Microsoft Excel or Google Spreadsheets. Such software is widely available and many people have at least basic experience with it. No special software or add ins are required. While the book assumes no knowledge of statistics, operations research, or management science, it does rely on basic familiarity with Excel.

The practical flavor of the book extends to chapter naming, which aims at conveying the purpose of each chapter. This naming convention slightly differs from the common practice in management science or statistics textbooks, where chapters are organized and named based on an analytical method, rather than a practical purpose.

Each chapter concludes with a set of exercises to encourage hands-on learning. From my experience, this the best way to master technical skills, and to really understand the approach and concepts explained in the chapter.

I would like to thank the people who have made this book come to fruition. I thank the Rigsum Institute's director Mr. Chen Chen Dorji for his pivotal role in organizing the workshops, and for his continuous support during the process of designing and refining the workshop as well as writing the book. The Rigsum faculty helped assure smooth and enjoyable workshops, relaxing my Western apprehension when things did not go as planned. I extend heartfelt thanks to Boaz Shmueli for his expert editorial and design advice and to Raquelle Azran for her professional and meticulous editing. Professor Inbal Yahav (University of Maryland) provided detailed comments and suggestions that improved the content and readability of the book. Peter Bruce (Statistics.com) offered valuable feedback and suggestions. Bhutan's Kuensel newspaper has graciously given me permission to reproduce several articles covering various projects in Bhutan. My thanks also to the many workshop participants from whom I learned much about project planning in Bhutan and its challenges. I also thank Ambient Café in Thimphu, for tolerating many hours of typing at their cafe and for supplying me with the needed caffeine and peace of mind for writing.

Galit Shmueli
October 2011

Project Planning, Data, and Spreadsheet Software

Project planning

DECISIONS HAVE IMPLICATIONS. Short-term or long-term, personal or public, decision making is a frequent and important occurrence. Decisions are based on a mixture of experience, domain knowledge and intuition. The purpose of this book is to show how experience and domain knowledge can be formalized to be better integrated into the decision making process involved in project planning. The use of data and software is in no way intended to replace the human expert or decision maker. On the contrary, they are useful tools that assist the decision maker in reaching a better understanding of both the big picture and its details.

We use the term *project* to refer to an investment of resources of any type for achieving a particular objective or set of objectives. This broad definition highlights the generality of the approach and methods presented in the book. Projects are undertaken by large and small organizations, in government, non-profits and businesses, and of course, by individuals. Determining whether to implement a project, or which project to implement among a set of possibilities is often a challenge with high stakes. Assessing the potential outcomes of a project under different scenarios is critically important. It is therefore useful to make informative decisions.

While the term *project planning* is broad and includes a variety of topics, the focus of this book is on project planning using *quantitative data*. In particular, it introduces scientific principles for assessing potential project performance and risk under different scenarios, by addressing uncertainty that arises at different levels. We also present approaches for comparing competing projects and reducing risk via project portfolios.

Data

THE FOCUS OF THIS BOOK is on how numerical data can be integrated into decision making at the project planning stage using spreadsheet software. By *data* we mean numerical data that are logically related to the decision or project of interest. We focus on numerical data because currently standard spreadsheet software is the most commonly used tool for storing, manipulating, and presenting numerical data. Numerical data are used to represent measurements related to projects, including factors affecting the project and the project outcomes. While there are many types of non-numerical data, such as text, images, audio and video, such non-numerical data can be converted into numerical form and used for project planning using the spreadsheet methods described in this book. For example, in verbal customer interviews that are intended to measure perception, the number of positive words and the number of negative words can be used as numerical indicators of positive and negative perception.

Spreadsheet software

SPREADSHEET SOFTWARE IS A POWERFUL AND DANGEROUS TOOL. When used wisely, it can simplify daunting tasks, help organize data and manipulate it effectively, and interact with the numbers. However, spreadsheet software can also be dangerous and misleading thanks to the same properties that make it powerful. One such feature of spreadsheet software, which distinguishes it from non-spreadsheet software, is the ability to use *cell references*, so that the values of some cells are calculations that are based on other cells. For example, the value in a certain cell can be the sum total of values of five other cells. The strength of cell references is that changing the referred cells automatically changes the referring cell. In the example shown in Figure 1, changing the value in one or more of the five cells will automatically affect the value of the sum total. The danger with cell references is that a spreadsheet can become overly complex, thereby leading to confusion regarding the relationship between the different cells. Another danger, when such a spreadsheet is printed out (as in a written report or presentation slides), is that it is impossible to know which cells are a function of other cells and which are not. There are several other properties of spreadsheet software that make it potent and potentially dangerous. The purpose of this book is to help you learn about strengths and pitfalls of spreadsheet software when used for decision making.

While Microsoft's Excel spreadsheet software is probably the most popular spreadsheet software in use today, the methods shown in this book and illustrated with Excel can be implemented with other spreadsheet software. One example is Google Spreadsheets (www.google.com/google-d-s/spreadsheets), which offers free online collaborative spreadsheet software (see Figure 1).

14

Figure 1: Spreadsheet
software showing cell
referencing. Top: Microsoft
Excel 2010. Bottom: Google
Spreadsheets

1   Why Plan?

WE OFTEN READ IN THE LOCAL NEWSPAPERS about projects
that end prematurely, are postponed or seriously delayed, or that
fail miserably. Although uncertainty is an inherent part of our
world, project planning can help reduce and quantify some uncertainty as well as predict the project outcomes under different
uncertain conditions. Investing time and energy in planning is
critical for improved outcomes and for making informed decisions.

Figure 1.1: Plan Ahead
cartoon

Let us consider a few recent examples from Bhutan. In August
2010, the Nepalese-based private airline Buddha Air started
operating flights between Bhutan and Kathmandu, Nepal. This
was the only airline flying from Kathmandu to Paro airport in
Bhutan aside from the national carrier Druk Air. After only two
weeks of operation, Buddha Air suspended operation due to
"heavy financial losses" as a result of very low occupancy on its
flights, and ceased operation on this route as of March 2011[1].
Another example of a project that was unexpectedly delayed

[1] As reported in Bhutan's
National Public Service
Broadcaster (BBS) on Feb
12, 2011 (www.bbs.com.bt/
bbs/?p=3736, accessed July
1, 2011).

HOME ✳ 3

Buddha Air

Operations suspended till Sept.13

Running at a complete loss in the Paro-K'mandu sector

GYALSTEN K DORJI, PARO

Two weeks after commencing commercial flights to Bhutan, Nepal-based Buddha air has suspended operations between the Paro-Kathmandu sector until September 13 because of heavy financial losses. The airline has not operated its last three scheduled flights into Paro.

▮ AVIATION

The airline has carried only 10 paying passengers between that only flights with no bookings had been cancelled. He said operations would recommence on 14 September.

As a scheduled operator, Buddha air has to inform the department of civil aviation (DCA) for any flight cancellations. DCA director general, Phala Dorji, said Buddha air has notified DCA of flight cancellations twice. He said that although DCA's perspective is that the airline be regular in their operations, the commercial aspect also needed to be taken into consideration.

Suspended: Not making money at all

Figure 1.2: Article from Bhutan's newspaper Kuensel, reporting the suspension of Buddha Air's flights to Bhutan

is the Centenary Farmers Market in Thimphu, which was inaugurated in October 2008. This project was aimed at upgrading the weekend vegetable market in the capital. During the construction period, which started in April 2007, vendors were relocated to an open football field, where sellers sat on the ground with no covering (see video at www.bhutanlink.com/thimphu-vegetable-market/). During the rainy season the area became muddy and quite unpleasant for both sellers and buyers. Everyone eagerly awaited the opening of the new market. However, once construction was complete and the market inaugurated, several months passed before the market became operational. The reason for the delay was an unexpected issue: demand for stalls was much higher than the 143 stalls that were operational during the first phase, thereby requiring a policy for allocating stalls to vendors. The chief environment office at the Thimphu City Corporation explained the delay "We're taking time because we want to ensure transparency and fairness in allotting the sheds to the vendors"[2]. It took more than a month to figure out a method for allocating stalls, and only then did the Centenary Farmers Market finally become operational[3].

[2] From Dec 1, 2008 Kuensel article www.kuenselonline.com/modules.php?name=News&file=article&sid=11550, accessed July 1, 2011

[3] See also the Oct 20, 2008 Kuensel article "Centennial Farmers Market : Inaugurated but wait a bit" kuenselonline.com/2010/modules.php?name=News&file=article&sid=11332, accessed July 1, 2011

Figure 1.3: Inauguration of the Centenary Farmers Market in Thimphu by Queen Ashi Dechen Yangzom Wangchuk in October 2008 (photo from www.moa.gov.bt, accessed July 1, 2011)

A third example of a large-scale project that, at the time of writing, is seeing unexpected challenges is the Thimphu Tech-Park. The aim of the project is to create Bhutan's first IT park, a "250,000 square ft IT-focused mixed use development spread over 18 acres" intended for IT office space and a data center. While construction has been progressing according to schedule, an unforeseen challenge has emerged: the search for an operator of the park has not been successful, and the two rounds of call-for-bids resulted in no bids at all.

Figure 1.4: Rendition of planned Thimphu TechPark, from www.thimphutechpark. com (accessed July 1, 2011)

The term *projects* can include initiatives beyond business projects. For example, government initiatives and new regulations can be considered projects that require planning and evaluation. Two examples in Bhutan are the January 2011 Tobacco Control Act that was passed by Parliament, and the June 2011 increased taxation on alcohol[4]. In both cases, the purpose of the regulation is to lower consumption of harmful substances. Whether the goal can be successfully achieved depends on various factors such as population awareness, population attitudes towards smoking and alcohol consumption, black-market availability, etc.

[4] For details on the increased taxation of alcohol see Bhutan's Ministry of Finance website www.mof.gov.bt

Smaller projects include the many newspapers and magazines that have mushroomed in the last few years. It is still debatable whether these endeavors have been successful in achieving their objectives.

Since many factors are uncontrollable and/or unpredictable,

is project planning futile? Are there ways to evaluate a project before it has been carried out? The answer is yes!

First, there are always key factors that are controllable to some extent. In the case of Buddha Air, pricing and marketing are two such factors. In the case of the Centenary Farmers Market, the number of stalls and the stall rental are two controllable factors. For the IT park, the operator requirements are controllable. In the alcohol taxation example, controllable factors include the new tax level, the date of implementation, and creating awareness campaigns. In the Tobacco Ban act, controllable factors are the repercussions for those violating the act, as mandated by law.

Second, some factors are predictable to some level. For Buddha Air, demand patterns on the Paro-Kathmandu line could be estimated from records of Druk Air, which has been operating on this line for many years. The Centenary Farmers Market could have predicted demand for stalls by estimating the number of vendors prior to the renovation and perhaps by surveying vendors during construction. For the Thimphu TechPark, operation costs can be roughly estimated using operation costs from other organizations. In the alcohol taxation case, the government can use estimates of current alcohol demand to predict possible levels of consumption once taxes are increased. It can also learn about the results of alcohol taxation in other countries that implemented similar measures. We can also incorporate our confidence in these numbers in a numerical fashion.

Finally, even for unpredictable and uncontrollable factors one can often evaluate the effect of unpredictable factors on the project by examining different possible scenarios (called *what-if* analysis) and sources of randomness. For example, Buddha Air could ask: *What if* the passenger rate is too low for the first three years?, *What if* fuel costs double in the next year?, *What if* the number of passengers varies randomly in a certain range?

In the following, we will consider these different sources of information that help reduce the uncertainty associated with a project before it has been carried out. We will see that even with a few numbers we can draw a general picture of different project outcomes under different scenarios. We will use spreadsheet software, and in particular Microsoft Excel (or you can use a spreadsheet software of your choice) to measure the effect of different factors and sources of uncertainty on the project outcomes.

2   Example: Ministry of Agriculture's Yoghurt Plant and Sales Project

To ILLUSTRATE THE PROCESS OF PROJECT PLANNING using Excel, we use a semi-realistic case study of a yoghurt production project. We base this example on the real yoghurt plant that was inaugurated by Bhutan's Ministry of Agriculture in September 2008. At the time, yoghurt was only produced by individuals and sold in some small shops. The Ministry of Agriculture decided to adopt a project for creating a yoghurt plant and selling yoghurt in Thimphu (and perhaps eventually outside of Thimphu). Based on this project, we create a fictitious, yet realistic, project planning scenario. In particular, we pretend to be in the year 2007, before a decision to launch the project has been made. We consider different factors that should affect the outcome of the yoghurt project, and evaluate performance over a 4-year horizon.

For the sake of simplicity, let us consider some factors that are controllable and others that are uncontrollable. In particular, for producing and selling yoghurt, we can consider the price of a yoghurt cup to be controllable by the Ministry of Agriculture. Pricing is obviously a non-trivial decision, because it is closely related to supply and demand, to competition, etc. Based on domain knowledge and market research, we can determine a price range that is reasonable. Another factor that is fairly controllable is the amount of yoghurt produced (within the limitation of milk availability, plant capacity, etc.). Here we must determine the minimum and maximum production amounts that are opera-

Figure 2.1: The yoghurt plant opened by the Ministry of Agriculture in Thimphu

tionally feasible and logical. Another important factor is the cost of producing a cup of yoghurt. This cost is affected by various factors such as wages, costs of raw materials and transportation, utility rates (e.g., power and water), and more. While production cost is clearly not completely controllable, we can determine a range of costs that, based on our experience and domain expertise, is reasonable. Finally, let us consider interest rates. This is an uncontrollable and hard-to-predict factor. We therefore must consult with financial experts, consider the time horizon of our evaluation, and then come up with a reasonable interest rate range (from lowest possible to highest possible). As you can see, project planning requires intensive use of domain expertise. It is not a matter of putting some numbers into a software program and getting answers. Instead, it is a process of formalizing and quantifying different factors by use of domain knowledge. Excel (or any software) will support us in extracting our domain knowledge and structuring it in a way that is easier to see the big picture, and to make informative decisions; the gathering of information is our first task.

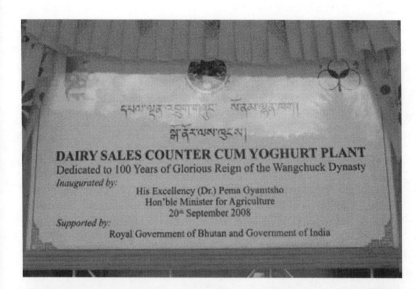

Figure 2.2: Inauguration of yoghurt plant and sales counter in Thimphu, September 2008

Exercises

1. Name three non-financial goals that the Ministry of Agriculture might be interested in achieving by executing the yoghurt project.

2. Name three factors that are likely to affect consumption of yoghurt in Thimphu, which would affect the yoghurt project.

3. In our example, we ignore fixed costs of setting up the plant. Name three resources that are likely to have fixed costs in the context of a yoghurt plant and sales project.

4. The Fortune Magazine article *Saving the World with a Cup of yogurt*[1] describes a yoghurt production project launched in 2006 in Bangladesh by the international Danone dairy company in collaboration with Grameen micro-financing. From the article:

   [1] The full article is available at money.cnn.com/magazines/fortune/fortune_archive/2007/02/05/8399198/ (accessed Sept 1, 2011)

   > "At a lunch in Paris, in the fall of 2005, Yunus invited Danone CEO Franck Riboud to come to Bangladesh and build his first social business enterprise. Riboud listened, then agreed. The yoghurt Danone would make would be fortified to help curb malnutrition and priced (at 7 cents a cup) to be affordable. All revenue from the joint venture with Grameen would be reinvested, with Danone (Charts) taking out only its initial cost of capital, about $500,000, after three years.
   >
   > The factory - and ultimately 50 more, if it works - will rely on Grameen microborrowers buying cows to sell it milk on the front end, Grameen microvendors selling the yoghurt door to door and Grameen's 6.6 million members purchasing it for their kids. It will employ 15 to 20 women.
   >
   > And Danone estimates that it will provide income for 1,600 people within a 20-mile radius of the plant. Biodegradable cups made from cornstarch, solar panels for electricity generation and rainwater collection vats make the enterprise environmentally friendly.
   >
   > International organizations such as Unicef believe it may be such a revolutionary means of improving nutrition through a sustainable business model that it is watching closely - and may seek to replicate around the world."

   (a) What are the main objectives of the Danone-Grameen yoghurt project?

(b) Is there any use in assessing the potential financial performance of this social project? Why?

(c) If Bhutan's Ministry of Agriculture decides to expand the yoghurt project for sale in rural areas of the country, what factors with financial implications must they factor into the spreadsheet?

3 *Defining Project Metrics*

3.1 *Defining goals*

To EVALUATE THE EFFECT OF DIFFERENT FACTORS on the project outcome, we must define performance measurements of interest. The metrics of interest depend on the goals of the project. Goals can be financial, social, combined, etc. They can be short-term or long-term. They can involve a single organization or a wide population. In the yoghurt project initiated by Bhutan's Ministry of Agriculture, goals can include improving the health of the local urban population, supporting local dairy farms by creating demand for milk products, providing more jobs (especially given the high youth unemployment rate in Thimphu), meeting consumer demand in the capital, or perhaps it is a financial venture which aims to generate profit for the government. In fact, several of these might be defined as the project goals. When several goals are defined, it is important to prioritize the goals and to define threshold values that can be defined as success.

3.2 *Defining metrics*

MOVING FROM GOAL DEFINITION TO PERFORMANCE EVALUATION requires defining relevant metrics for input factors and for the project outcome. While financial metrics are the most common in project planning, one should carefully consider other metrics of success. In construction projects, for instance, a relevant metric is usually time to completion, or timeliness. Delays in completion time can cause major disruptions and inconvenience and therefore usually lead to fines and other repercussions to the construction agency.

Customer satisfaction and building a firm's reputation are common goals. Public IT, media, and telecommunication organizations (such as TV and radio channels) often launch new programs that are intended to be of interest to their audience. Satisfaction is commonly assessed using customer satisfaction surveys. Such surveys, if carefully designed and carried out, help measure the success of a project in the eyes of the intended audience.

When measuring the health benefits of a project, metrics of interest can include rate of hospitalization, or of related outcomes. For example, in the alcohol taxation case, metrics of project success can include the rate of road accidents due to alcohol, and the rate of alcohol-related diseases as observed in hospitals and basic health units.

Financial metrics are often of interest, even when the main purpose of the project is not money-making. Governmental and non-profit organizations must also maintain financial feasibility to use their funds effectively. In such cases, financial measures might be used as secondary measures, to evaluate the potential financial risks of an intended project. Because of the importance of financial metrics and capital budgeting in the majority of projects, we introduce the common financial metric of *net present value* (NPV). This metric measures the value that a project or investment adds to the organization (or shareholders). NPV compares the gains from investing in a certain project to an alternative investment that yields a given rate of return (ROR) (also known as *return on investment* (ROI)). For example, we can compare to the alternative of leaving the money in the bank and gaining interest. Or, if implementing the project requires taking a loan, the rate of return that we compare to is (at least) the loan rate.

In addition to a required rate of return, computing NPV requires estimating the project's cash flows. We treat all of these (including the rate of return) as *input factors*. NPV is computed by adding up the yearly terms

$$\text{Value for year } t = \frac{\text{cash flow in year } t}{(1 + \text{rate of return})^t} \qquad (3.1)$$

In Section 3.4 we will see how to compute this metric step by step. For now, let us illustrate the notions of *input factors* and *outcome measure* for the yoghurt plant example. We consider four input factors:

1. *Price per unit*: the price of a yoghurt cup is set at Nu 20 (based on an initial pricing estimate). *Nu* is the Bhutanese currency abbreviation, for *ngultrum*.

2. *Cost per unit*: we set the cost of producing a yoghurt cup at Nu 5 (taking into account labor, materials, utilities, etc.)

3. *Units produced*: the amount of production is set at 12,000 cups in the first year of the project and 20,000 cups per year thereafter (based on operational feasibility).

4. *Rate of return*: set at 7% annually (based on bank interest rates in Bhutan in 2007).

And we consider one particular *outcome measure* of interest here, which is NPV (the financial value of the yoghurt project to the Ministry of Agriculture). Of course in reality we might have multiple *outcome measures* of interest, with some having higher priority than others.

3.3   Setting up a spreadsheet

Organizing inputs and outcomes on the spreadsheet

Let us compute the NPV over the 4-year horizon 2008-2011, as a factor of the input factors. To do this, we create a new Excel spreadsheet. We start by placing the input factors that do not change over the 4-year period at the top (see Figure 3.1). In column B we type the factor names, and in column C we type the respective values. In our example, we include *price per unit*, *cost per unit*, and *interest rate* at the top (cells B1-B3). Below these factors, we create a table that includes a column for each year within our 4-year horizon. In our example, the factor *units pro-duced* changes from year to year and is therefore included in the yearly table.

	A	B	C	D	E	F
1		Price per unit	BTN 20			
2		Cost per unit	BTN 5			
3		Interest rate	7%			
4						
5			2008	2009	2010	2011
6		Year				
7		Units produced	12,000	20,000	20,000	20,000

Figure 3.1: Organizing a spreadsheet with input factors. At the top are factors that are fixed during the entire period. Below are factors that change over the project horizon

Next, we include the information that we already have in the relevant cells in the spreadsheet. The information given for our example is the *price per unit* (Nu 20), *cost per unit* (Nu 5), *interest rate* (7%), and *units produced* (12,000 cups in 2008, then 20,000 cups per year thereafter).

Formatting cells

It is important to format the values that we entered in their appropriate units. For example, both *price* and *cost* are in units of ngultrum (Nu), and interest rate is a percentage. While we can simply type "Nu 20" in the cell (C1 in our example), this will cause Excel to treat the cell as text rather than a numerical value, thereby not allowing us to perform any numerical operations on it. Spreadsheet software such as Excel allows us to include cell information such as currency, unit, etc. by formatting the cell of interest. How is this done? First type the numerical value 20 in cell C1. Now, use the *format cells* option (available by right-clicking on the cell). You will see a menu that allows you to choose various formats, including number formats, currencies, date formats, and more. The screenshot in Figure 3.2 shows the *Format Cells* menu.

Click on *Currency*. You will find all the popular currencies there[1] (such as $). For lesser used currencies (such as Nu), scroll to the very bottom of the currency list and you will find 3-letter currency codes for all available currencies. In the case of Bhutanese ngultrum (Nu), if it does not exist, you can use the

[1] The types of currencies that you will find in the *Format Cells* menu depend on the option chosen during Windows installation. You can change these defaults in the *Clock, Language, and Region* area of the Control Panel (click *Additional Settings*).

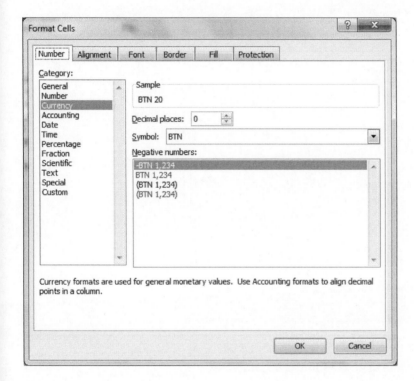

Figure 3.2: Excel's *Format Cells* menu (right-click on a cell to find this menu). BTN is the 3-letter code for Bhutan's currency (Nu)

3-letter code BTN. In this example, we will work in rounded Nu figures and we choose to display 0 decimals for currency.

Finally, make sure that the interest rate value 7 is formatted as a percentage. You can try typing "7%" but then open the *Format Cells* menu to make sure that Excel recognizes this as a percentage (see Figure 3.3).

Figure 3.3: Formatting a cell as a percentage

Next, we use the input numbers to compute costs, revenues, and profit.

Computing costs

For the sake of simplicity, we ignore any fixed costs (for example, for purchase of machinery) and base variable costs only on the "cost-per-unit" numbers. We perform the computations using the spreadsheet's formulas, thereby creating cells references. This will allow us to later change the value for *cost per unit* and the variable costs cells will automatically update accordingly. In our example, variable costs for year 2008 are the *cost per unit* for each of the 12,000 units produced. This gives a total of Nu 5*12000 = Nu 60000. Let us include this figure in cell C8. Instead of typing this number, we will use Excel's multiplication formula and refer to cell C2 (*cost per unit*) and cell C7 (*units produced* in 2008).

Absolute cells and relative cells

One option for obtaining the 60,000 figure in cell C8 is to type the formula[2] =C7*C2. This will yield the correct number and will create a cell reference. However, if we use this formula, computing the variable costs for years 2009, 2010, and 2011 will require creating three additional formulas. Why? What will happen if we simply copy the formula to the cells of the following years? Try it! You will find that for year 2009 the formula will be multiplying cell D7 (*units produced* in 2008) by D2, which is an empty cell, instead of by C2. This occurs because by default Excel uses *relative cells*. When you click *Copy* from the menu, Excel does not only copy the formula but also the position of the cells referenced in the formula, relative to the C8 cell, which contains the formula. If you copy the function across rows or down columns, the reference automatically adjusts.

> [2] Note that the equal sign (=) must precede any Excel formula. While =C7*C2 multiplies the values in cells C7 and C2, typing C7*C2 will simply create text and not compute anything

A more efficient (and less error-prone) approach is to utilize Excel's absolute cells option. An absolute cell reference in a formula, such as $A$1, always refers to a cell in a specific location. If the position of the cell that contains the formula changes, the absolute reference remains unchanged. In our example, we want to fix *cost per unit* to be read only from cell C2. This is done by referring to C2 as an absolute cell. To do this, instead of typing C2 in our formula, we type $C$2. The formula would therefore be =C7*$C$2. Now, when copying this formula to years 2009 on, *cost per unit* will be read from cell C2, while *units produced* will be read from the appropriate relative cells (D7 for year 2008, E7 for year 2009, and F7 for year 2010).

Cell names

Another good approach to computing formulas, which can be copied to other rows or columns, is to use cell naming. Instead

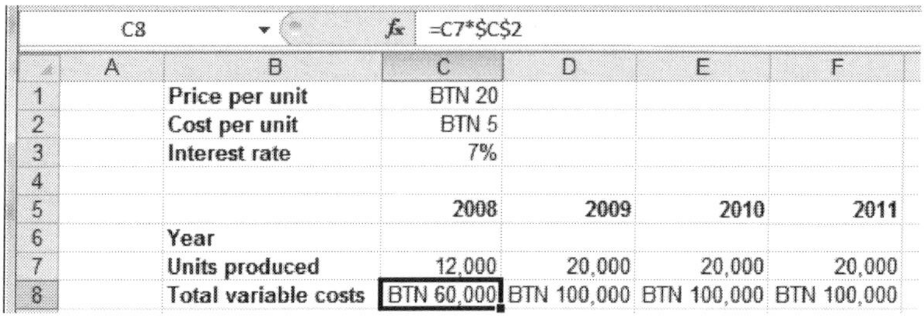

Figure 3.4: Using absolute and relative cell reference in computing variable costs

of referencing a cell by its location (such as C2), we can give it a name. When we reference the cell name in a formula, it acts like an absolute cell reference. Naming a cell also makes it easier to reference the right cell, if the name is meaningful.

For example, we can name cell C2 "cost". To do this, we type "cost" in the name box that appears at the top left of the worksheet (see Figure 3.5). The word "cost" is now the name of cell C2 in this entire worksheet. We can do the same to name the price-per-unit and interest rate numbers (cells C1 and C3). To modify or remove names, use the *Name Manager* in the *Formulas* tab. Now that cell C2 is named "cost", we can compute the 2008 variable cost figure using the formula =C7*cost.

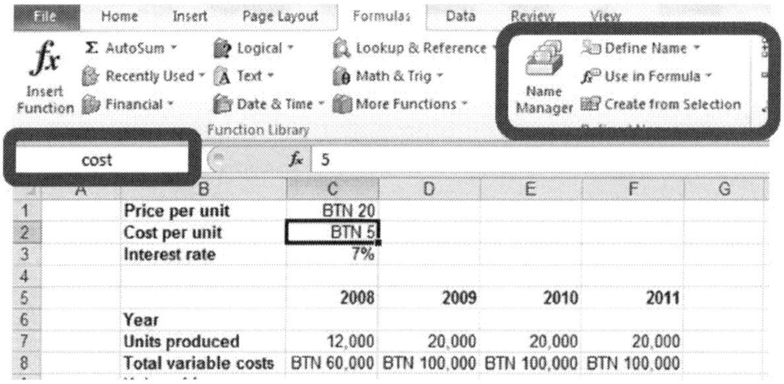

Figure 3.5: Assigning the name "cost" to cell C2, by typing in the Name Box. Managing names (changing, removing, etc.) can be done from the Name Manager menu (under Formulas tab)

Computing revenues and profit

To compute revenues, there is one detail that is still missing, namely, the number of units sold each year. Because we do not have this information at the time of project planning (recall that we assume that it is now year 2007), we will use projected numbers. As we did with other inputs, we will use our domain knowledge to come up with estimates, and then we can modify these values to see how different levels affect the project outcome. For now, let us assume a "worst case" demand scenario[3] for the Ministry of Agriculture's new yoghurt product, where they will sell only 1,000 cups in the first year, 10,000 cups in the second year, and 12,000 cups per year thereafter (note that the projected annual sales cannot exceed the annual number of units produced). We add this *units sold* information to our spreadsheet table in row 9, as shown in Figure 3.6.

[3] These numbers can be modified later to reflect more favorable demand scenarios. We will also look at demand as a function of price in Section 4.3

	A	B	C	D	E	F
1		Price per unit	BTN 20			
2		Cost per unit	BTN 5			
3		Interest rate	7%			
4						
5			2008	2009	2010	2011
6		Year				
7		Units produced	12,000	20,000	20,000	20,000
8		Total variable costs	BTN 60,000	BTN 100,000	BTN 100,000	BTN 100,000
9		Units sold	1000	10,000	12,000	12,000

Figure 3.6: Adding projected demand for each of the four years ("units sold")

Given the projected demand (*units sold*), we now have all the numbers needed to compute revenue, profit, and finally net present value (NPV). To compute revenue, we once again use Excel's formulas and combine relative and absolute references. In particular, the revenue for a certain year is equal to the number of units sold times the price of a single unit. If we name cell C1 as "price", then our revenue formula for year 2008 (which we input in cell C10) can be typed as *=price*C9*. Alternatively, we can use absolute reference to the price-per-unit value $C$1. We can then copy the formula to the revenue sales in years 2009-2011, as shown in Figure 3.7. Next, we compute annual profit. This is done by subtracting the variable costs from the revenue for that year. The formula for year 2008 is therefore *=C10-C8*. Here too, we can copy the 2008 profit value from cell C11 to cells D11, E11, and F11, corresponding to Profit in years 2009-2011.

	A	B	C	D	E	F
			C15 ▼ (f_x =NPV(C3,C11:F11)			
1		Price per unit	BTN 20			
2		Cost per unit	BTN 5			
3		Interest rate	7%			
4						
5			2008	2009	2010	2011
6		Year	1	2	3	4
7		Units produced	12,000	20,000	20,000	20,000
8		Total variable costs	BTN 60,000	BTN 100,000	BTN 100,000	BTN 100,000
9		Units sold	1000	10,000	12,000	12,000
10		Revenues	BTN 20,000	BTN 200,000	BTN 240,000	BTN 240,000
11		Profit	-BTN 40,000	BTN 100,000	BTN 140,000	BTN 140,000
12		Present value	-BTN 37,383	BTN 87,344	BTN 114,282	BTN 106,805
13						
14		Net Present Value	BTN 271,048			
15		Excel's NPV function	BTN 271,048			

Figure 3.7: Spreadsheet complete with input factor information, derived calculations, and outcome measure NPV

3.4 Computing Financial Metrics

Net Present Value (NPV)

Next, we'd like to sum up our profit numbers over the horizon of the interest (in this case, four years). However, because of the interest rate, figures for different years are not on the same scale. For example, Nu 100,000 of today is not the same as Nu 100,000 in two years. Therefore, we must scale all the profit figures so that they reflect "today's value". In other words, we are discounting the cash flow for its present value. To do this, we must take into account interest rate. To compute *present value* for a certain year, we must have three pieces of information:

1. The profit in that year (*profit*)

2. How far into the future that year is (that is, how many years from now? (*years*)

3. What is the interest rate? (*rate*)

Given these three numbers, the Present Value for a given year is

$$\text{Present Value} = \frac{\text{profit}}{(1+\text{rate})^{\text{years}}} \qquad (3.2)$$

For the year 2008, for instance, we compute the present value as

$$\text{Present value}(2008) = \frac{-40,000}{(1+0.07)^1} = \text{Nu} - 37383 \qquad (3.3)$$

In Excel, we can compute this easily by adding a row named *year* or *years*, with value 1 for year 2008, value 2 for year 2009, etc. (see Figure 3.7). Then, *Present Value* is computed using the above formula with relative reference to profit and year and absolute reference to interest rate. For year 2008, we can use the Excel formula *=C11 / (1+$C$3)^C6*. Note that computing a power in Excel can be done by using the sign ^, such that a^b means "a to the power of b". Alternatively, the function *=power(a,b)* can be used.

The last step is adding the Present Value numbers from each year to obtain the NPV. Hence, we use the function *=sum(C12:F12)*.

We can also use a shortcut in computing NPV. After computing the annual profit numbers, we can simply use Excel's function *=npv(rate,profits)*. The first argument in the function is the interest rate. The second is the list of profits in year 1,2, 3, etc. In our example, we would use the function as follows: *=npv($C$3,C11:F11)*. This function yields the same number as the manual calculation that we performed earlier (where we computed annual present value numbers and then added them up).

Internal Rate of Return (IRR)

While the focus of this book is not on financial performance, we will also mention the *internal rate of return* (IRR), which is a popular financial metric often used in conjunction with NPV in private equity investments. Both NPV and IRR are used to measure and compare the profitability of investments. Both NPV and IRR will always agree on whether a project increases or decreases in value.

The IRR gives us, for a given set of annual profits, the rate of return that sets the NPV to zero. In other words, it is the rate of return where the present value of the cash flow equals the project's initial investment. The higher a project's IRR, the more desirable it is to undertake the project. Unlike NPV, which indicates the magnitude of an investment, the IRR is a rate which indicates the efficiency of the investment.

Excel's function IRR can easily compute the IRR, given a set of annual profits. In our example, we can compute the IRR by $=irr(C11:F11)$. We obtain a very large value of IRR=270%. It means that the project must earn a return rate of 270% to balance cash flows with initial investment. This huge value is due to the fact that we omitted fixed costs, such as initial investment in machinery, from the calculation. Such initial costs would be included in our spreadsheet as "year 0", thereby adding another column for year 2007.

In summary, we computed the *net present value* using data on pricing, costs, projected demand and interest rate. These are sufficient for computing financial measures such as NPV. Although we focused on NPV, it is important to note that we could have performed a similar spreadsheet calculation for other metrics of interest, such as time to completion, overall satisfaction, etc.

We have demonstrated how to set up a spreadsheet with inputs that are fixed throughout the project period of interest and with inputs that vary. We looked at spreadsheet functions, relative and absolute cells, cell naming, cell formatting, and more. Using such operations will help us to easily evaluate the effect of modifying the input values on the outcome measurements of interest, as we will see in the next section.

Exercises

A 2005 article in the Kuensel newspaper entitled *'Egg-cellent' business*[4] describes the following business supplying local eggs:

[4] The article is available online at kuenselonline.com/ 2010/modules.php?name= News&file=article&sid= 5853

> "The Satara farm in Langjophakha supplies about 40 cartons (8,400) of local eggs a week to numerous grocery stores in Thimphu. Established in 2000 with 250 birds, the farm today has about 500 birds and earns more than Nu 700 a day.
>
> According to proprietor Drimi Wangda, they collect about 400 eggs each day and a tray of 30 eggs is sold for Nu 130.
>
> While the business was profitable, it required hard work according to Drimi Wangda. "The birds are delicate creatures and their maintenance and the feeds need extra attention," he said.
>
> The birds are given de-worming tablets every two months and vaccinated once in three months. "The chicken feed is the most expensive," he said. "A kilogramme costs Nu. 13 and more than 700 kilogrammes is required in a month."

1. Create a spreadsheet for computing the annual profit for the Satara farm. Include the number of eggs, sale price of an egg, and feed cost. Format each cell properly.

2. In your spreadsheet, which cells are absolute and which are relative?

3. Suppose that you are considering starting a similar poultry farm in the capital. Use the figures from Satara's case to compute the NPV over a three year horizon. Assume that cost, price and demand remain constant over the three years, assume a one time capital expenditure of Nu 100,000, and assume that you must take a loan at 12% interest rate.[5]

[5] See a real example of cost calculations for planning a layer poultry farm for 2000 birds in India at www.nabard.org/ modelbankprojects/animal_ layer.asp (Annexure II)

4. How does the NPV change if the monthly cost of feed increases by Nu 2 per kg?

5. How does the NPV change if a tray is sold for Nu 150?

6. If the government undertakes a similar project for the purpose of improving nutrition, what is the lowest sale price per egg (round up to the nearest ngultrum) that would still make the project financially viable (non-negative NPV) over 3 years? Assume a return rate of 12% and production costs as described above.

4   *Scenario Building*

NOW THAT WE HAVE CREATED A SPREADSHEET that links the input factors to the outcome measurements of interest, we can start evaluating the impact of different factors. In particular, let us look at the effect of:

1. Price of a cup, which we vary between Nu 10 and Nu 40,

2. Cost of producing a cup: Based on various costs (labor, materials, utilities), we consider the cost range Nu 3 to Nu 5, and

3. Return rate: Based on financial projections of interest rate, we look at the range 5%-7%.

Another input factor that we keep fixed (only for simplicity!) is the amount of production. We set this to 12,000 cups in the first year (year 2007) and 20,000 cups per year thereafter. Of course, we can use the same approach later on for varying the levels of this factor, as well as demand levels.

4.1   *Manipulating an input factor: Data Tables*

Let us start by asking how pricing affects NPV. We could do this manually by modifying the value in the spreadsheet (cell C1 in our spreadsheet) and examine the resulting NPV. This approach is not only inefficient, as it requires repetitive operations, but it also does not allow us to easily see the larger picture of the relationship between pricing and projected NPV. A better approach is to use Excel's *One Way Data Table*. This tool gives a table of an outcome of interest, computed for different values of a single input factor. Figure 4.1 shows an example of a One Way Table for NPV as a function of *price per unit*[1]. We can see how NPV changes quite drastically when the price of a yoghurt cup moves between Nu 10 and 30: from a negative value for a pricing of Nu 10 to nearly 600,000 for a pricing of Nu 30. We see that NPV is expected to be negative for a pricing of Nu 10 but positive for the other values. In addition, increases of Nu 5 in the yoghurt price are associated with jumps of around Nu 150,000 in NPV, in the explored pricing range. In short, we see that a table displaying the relations between an input factor and the measured outcome can be quite informative.

[1] Here we make a simplifying assumption that *units produced* are independent of price. In Section 4.3 we examine the more realistic case where demand depends on pricing

price per unit	BTN 10	BTN 15	BTN 20	BTN 25	BTN 30
BTN 279,704	-BTN 14,536	BTN 132,584	BTN 279,704	BTN 426,823	BTN 573,943

Figure 4.1: Excel's One Way Table is used for exploring the effect of Price on NPV

To create this table, start by creating a table with two rows, which has the values of price that you want to explore in the top row, as shown in Figure 4.2. We chose to explore the price values of Nu 10, 15, 20, 25, and 30 but any other values could have been used. The left-most cell in the second row should contain the formula of the outcome metric of interest (you can actually compute more than one outcome metric by using more rows). In our example, we used the formula =C15 which gives the NPV computation.

price per unit	BTN 10	BTN 15	BTN 20	BTN 25	BTN 30
BTN 279,704					

Figure 4.2: First, create a table with value of Price that you want to explore

Next, highlight the table area, go to *Data Tools > What-If Analysis*, and choose *Data Table*. Since we created a "row table" (where the input values for *price per unit* are listed in a row), we must tell Excel the location of the price value, which it will then "modify" to compute the new NPVs. This is entered in *Row input cell* in the *Data Table* menu. In our example, the location is cell C1 (see Figure 4.3). Excel now "inserts" each of the price values from our table into cell C1, and "collects" the resulting NPV values into our table. Clicking OK will give us the completed table shown in Figure 4.1.

Instead of a "row table", we can generate a "column table", where the values of the input factor are listed in the first column (instead of the first row). Then, use the *Column input cell* in the Data Table menu. Note that the row table and the column table allow us to explore the effect of a single input factor on one or more outcome measurements.

	A	B	C	D	E	F	G
1		Price per unit	BTN 20				
2		Cost per unit	BTN 5				
3		Interest rate	7%				
4							
5			2008	*Data Table*		11	
6		Year	1			4	
7		Units produced	12,000	Row input cell: $C$1		00	
8		Total variable costs	BTN 60,000	Column input cell:		00	
9		Units sold	1000			00	
10		Revenues	BTN 20,000	OK Cancel		00	
11		Profit	-BTN 40,000			00	
12		Present value	-BTN 37,383			05	
13							
14		Net Present Value	BTN 271,048				
15		Excel's NPV function	BTN 271,048				
16							
17							
18		price per unit	BTN 10	BTN 15	BTN 20	BTN 25	BTN 30
19		BTN 271,048					
20							

Figure 4.3: Top: Data Tables in Excel 2007 and 2010 are in Data Tools > What-If Analysis. Bottom: For a row-table, use only Row input cell

To explore the effect of changing two input factors, we can use Excel's *Two Way Data Table*. As before, we create a table with the levels of the first input factor listed in the top row, and the levels of the second input factor listed in the left-most column. In the top-left cell, we enter the formula for computing the outcome measurement of interest. In our case, to compute NPV we again use $=C15$. After highlighting the table (as shown in Figure 4.4), we fill both *Row input cell* and *Column input cell* in the *Data Table* menu. In our example, we have *price* in rows and hence choose cell C1 for *Row input cell*. We have *rate* in columns and therefore choose cell C3 for Column input cell.

4.2   *Manipulating multiple input factors: Scenario Manager*

In the last section we saw that one-way data tables can be used for exploring the effect of a single input factor on the outcome

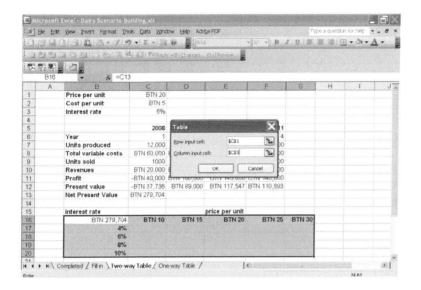

Figure 4.4: Two-way tables allow exploring two input factors. Values of one input factor (Price) are listed in the top row, and of the other factor (Interest rate) are in the left-most column. Highlight only the area shown to use Excel's Data Table.

measure(s) of interest. Two-way data tables allow the exploration of two input factors simultaneously. By varying more than one factor at a time, we get a clearer picture of the different possible scenarios that can occur in terms of the input factors. Recall that input factors can be controllable, uncontrollable but predictable, or uncontrollable and unpredictable. Exploring the outcome measure(s) under different scenarios of input variables of the different types can therefore give decision makers a better understanding of the possible outcomes under different decisions and under different uncontrollable conditions.

To explore the outcome as a function of more than two input factors, we can use Excel's *Scenario Manager*. This tool requires the user to set up a set of scenarios of interest, and then evaluates the outcome measure(s) under those scenarios. To illustrate Scenario Manager, let us explore the effect of three input factors: the controllable factor *price*, the less-controllable but somewhat predictable factor *cost*, and the even less predictable factor *rate*. We must first determine reasonable ranges of values for each of the factors, based on experience, historic data and expertise (financial, marketing, operational, and other related expertise). Let us assume that reasonable pricing of a yoghurt cup for the

Thimphu market is somewhere between Nu. 10-30. The cost is projected to range between Nu. 3-7, and bank interest rates between 4-8%. Let us consider two extreme scenarios:

Best-case Scenario: In terms of NPV, the best case is when selling price is high, production cost is low, and rate is low. Hence, the best-case scenario values are *price=30, cost=3, rate=4%*.

Worst-case Scenario: Using the same logic, the worst case values are *price=10, cost=5, rate=8%*.

Evaluating NPV in these two scenarios can be done manually, by plugging in the values of price, cost, and rate in our spreadsheet (cells C1,C2,C3 in our example) and observing the NPV cell (C14). There are three disadvantages to this manual process:

1. We cannot easily compare and contrast the NPVs from the different scenarios, unless we copy each NPV into a new area on the spreadsheet.

2. If we have many scenarios, the process becomes tedious and error-prone. It will also be hard to detect errors, because there will be no trace of the values that we entered.

3. We cannot easily integrate the resulting NPVs in further computations (as we will see in the next section).

Excel's *Scenario Manager* offers a tool that overcomes these three problems. It automatically computes the outcome metrics of interest for each of a set of scenarios that the user specifies, and displays all the input and outcome information for each scenario in one place. Figure 4.5 shows the output of *Scenario Manager* for the two scenarios mentioned above, based on the yoghurt project spreadsheet. We can see that the projected NPV ranges between Nu 609,453 in the best case scenario and -133,389 (note the negative sign) in the worst case.

To use the *Scenario Manager*, place your cursor in the spreadsheet that contains the input and outcome values. Then go to *Data Tools > What-If Analysis* and choose *Scenario Manager*. The first step is to create the scenarios of interest. Click *Add*. Name the scenario, preferably using a meaningful scenario name, and

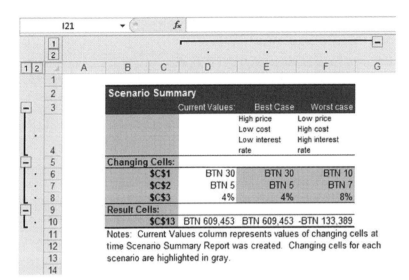

Figure 4.5: Scenario Manager summary output for two scenarios (Best Case and Worst Case). For each scenario the values of price, cost, and rate are set by the user. NPV is computed by Excel for each scenario.

choose the cells on the spreadsheet where the input values should be entered (in our example, C1:C3, as shown in Figure 4.6). It is helpful to add a comment explaining what this scenario means and any other useful details. Once all the scenarios of interest are entered, click *Summary* to obtain the NPV value for each scenario, as shown in Figure 4.5.

In Chapter 5 we will see how the results from *Scenario Manager* can be integrated into computations that take into account the risk associated with each scenario.

4.3   Linking input factors

Thus far, we treated each input factor independent of other input factors, entering into the spreadsheet values or formulas that are independent of other input factors. Often, an input factor will depend on other input factors. For example, projected sales of yoghurt are likely to depend on pricing. Similarly, production cost often depends on the amount produced. In the case of Buddha Air, occupancy levels are affected by airfare, time of year, and perception of safety. In the Centenary Farmers Market case, demand for stalls might depend on stall location as well as on

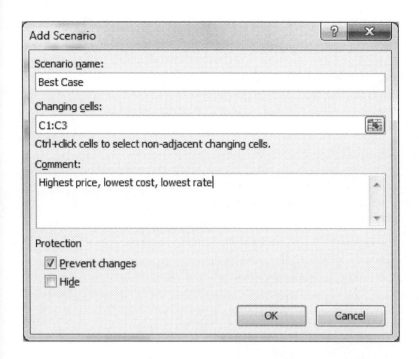

Figure 4.6: Adding a new scenario in Scenario Manager requires naming the scenario and entering the range of cells where the input values are located. In our example, we are entering values for cost, price, and rate, which go into cells C_1, C_2, C_3

season. Such relationships between input factors must be taken into account, as they are likely to affect the outcome. Next, we introduce several approaches for linking measurements, using the *if* function, lookup tables and using curves.

"If" Function

In some cases, we may have a list of pairs of numbers that link values of one input factor to another. In the yoghurt plant example, the cost of producing a yoghurt cup is likely to depend on the amount of production, such that the cost decreases as production increases. If there are only a few cost levels or there exists a simple formula for computing one factor from the other, we can use Excel's *=if* function. The structure of the function is *=if(condition, true, false)*. If the condition is satisfied, then the function returns the *true* value, and otherwise it returns the *false* value. For instance, *=if(5>3,1,2)* returns the value 1, because the condition $5 > 3$ is true (5 is indeed larger than 3).

We can also use multiple *if* functions, one within the other, to accommodate more than two possible values. For instance, if production cost is Nu 5 per cup below 10,000 cups, Nu 4 between 10,000-15,000 cups and Nu 3 above 15,000 cups, and our *amount produced* number is in cell C7, then we can compute the cost using

$$=if(C7<10000,5,if(C7<15000,4,3)).$$

Lookup Tables

With more than three values, the use of the *if* function becomes cumbersome. With several values and no simple formula relating the two input factors, we can summarize the information in a few Excel columns, and then "lookup" values in the table. An example is shown in Figure 4.7. Columns H-I show the production cost for three levels of production. Cells C2:F2 then use Excel's *=lookup* function to calculate *cost per unit* based on the amount of production in a given year (cells C7:F7).

	C2	▾	f_x =LOOKUP(C7,$H$2:$H$4,$I$2:$I$4)					
	A	B	C	D	E	F	G	H	I
1		Price per unit	BTN 15					minimum produced	cost
2		Cost per unit	BTN 5	BTN 3	BTN 3	BTN 3		0	BTN 5
3		Interest rate	4%					15,000	BTN 4
4								20,000	BTN 3
5			2008	2009	2010	2011			
6		Year	1	2	3	4			
7		Units produced	12,000	20,000	20,000	20,000			
8		Total variable costs	BTN 60,000	BTN 100,000	BTN 100,000	BTN 100,000			
9		Units sold	1000	10,000	12,000	12,000			
10		Revenues	BTN 15,000	BTN 150,000	BTN 180,000	BTN 180,000			
11		Profit	-BTN 45,000	BTN 50,000	BTN 80,000	BTN 80,000			
12		Present value	-BTN 43,269	BTN 46,228	BTN 71,120	BTN 68,384			
13		Net Present Value	BTN 142,463						

Figure 4.7: Using Excel's *=loopkup* function to link *cost per unit* to *units produced*

The *=lookup* function looks for a value of interest in one column and returns the value in the same row in another column. In the example shown in Figure 4.7, *=if(15,000,H2:H5,I2:I5)* will look for the value 15,000 in cells H2:H5 (the production amounts), and will then return Nu 4 (cost)[2]. We therefore use *=if(C7,H2:H5,I2:I5)* to compute *cost per unit* for year 2008 (C7 is the amount produced in year 2008) and replace C7 in the formula with D7, E7, and F7 for each of the following years.

[2] Note: If the *lookup* function cannot find the specified value, the function matches the largest value that is less than or equal to specified value. For instance *=if(17,000,H2:H5,I2:I5)* also returns Nu 4. Although 17,000 does not exist in column H, the largest value that is less than or equal to 17,000 is 15,000.

Curves

We will now discuss a method for devising formulas that capture a relationship between input factors (or in general, between any two measurements). The idea is to use a graphic representation of the relationship and then find the formula that describes that graphic representation, and include it in the spreadsheet. We illustrate this through *demand curves*, although the idea can be easily generalized to a relationship between any two measurements of interest.

A *demand curve* is a graph depicting the relationship between the price of a certain commodity, and the amount of it that consumers are willing and able to purchase at that given price. On the graph, *price* is drawn on the horizontal axis and *demand* (the number of units sold) on the vertical axis. Building a *demand curve* is an attempt to approximate the effect of pricing on demand.

Linear Relationship

The simplest demand curve is a straight line, indicating a linear relationship between price and demand. Fitting a linear relationship indicates that we believe that an increment of, say, Nu 1 in price will affect demand equally whether the increase in the price of a yoghurt cup is from Nu 10 to Nu 11 or from Nu 20 to Nu 21. When such an assumption is unreasonable or if we have data that support a different (more complex) type of relationship, we can fit a non-linear curve.

A linear demand curve can be estimated if we can specify two pairs of price and demand values. Let us assume that from market research of existing yoghurt sales in Thimphu, we know that pricing a cup at Nu 5 will sell the entire capacity that our plant can produce (12,000 in the first year and 20,000 per year thereafter). We also know that pricing a cup at Nu 30 will sell only around 3,300 cups a year. Using these two data points (price=5, demand=20,000) and (price=30, demand=3,300) we can estimate a linear demand curve for years 2009 on, as shown in Figure 4.10.

Generating a straight line (a linear model) in Excel is straightforward: Create a column with the two prices of interest (5 and 30) and a column of the corresponding demand (20,000 and 3,300), as shown in the left of Figure 4.10. Highlight the two columns and click *Insert > Charts > Scatter* and choose the top-left chart (see Figure 4.8). Now, click on the chart once, and in the *Chart Layout* menu click the *Trendlines* arrow and choose *Linear Trendline*. This will automatically fit a straight line through the two points that you specified.

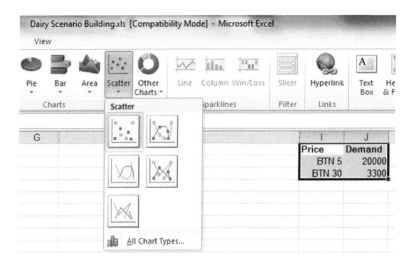

Figure 4.8: Creating a linear demand curve from price and demand columns: Highlight the columns and choose a scatter chart

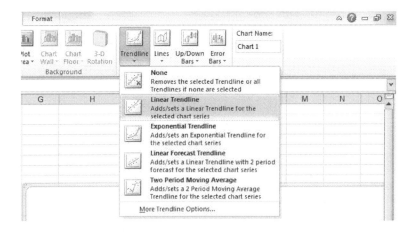

Figure 4.9: Creating a linear curve is done by using the Chart Layout > Analysis > Trendline tool

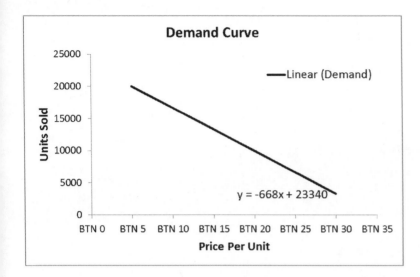

Figure 4.10: Linear demand curve for yoghurt project

Finally, we want to find the formula that the linear demand curve depicts, so that we can build the relationship between *price* and *units sold* into our worksheet. To find the formula, select the chart, then click *Chart Tools > Layout > Trendlines* and choose *More Trendline Options*. In the window that opens click *Display Equation on chart* (see Figure 4.11). The linear equation is now shown on the plot near the straight line, as shown in Figure 4.10. It is given by

$$units\,sold = -668 price + 23340.$$

To integrate the linear demand curve into our spreadsheet, we replace the values in the *units sold* row with a formula. We must also make sure not to "sell" more units that are produced in that year. Hence, we will cap the units sold at the appropriate *units produced* cell. For example, for year 2008, we will cap it at the number in cell C7 (12,000 units). The formula for year 2008 is therefore =MIN(-668*$C$1 + 23340, C7). This formula can then be copied to years 2009-2011.

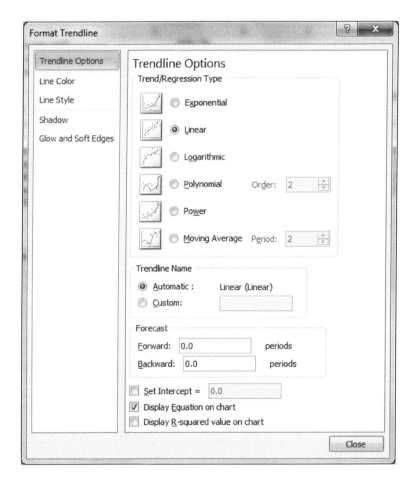

Figure 4.11: Creating a linear curve is done by using the Chart Layout > Analysis > Trendline tool

Non-Linear Relationships

If a linear relationship does not properly describe the relationship between the two measurements of interest, we can make use of a few more flexible types of relationships, again using trendlines. Two very popular relationships (based on empirical usefulness) are exponential and quadratic relationships. In exponential relationships, roughly speaking, a unit increase in the x-axis is associated with a percentage increase in the y-axis. Exponential relationships are a popular choice for demand curves.

To create such an exponential demand curve, follow the same steps as in the linear demand curve, but choose *Exponential* in the Trendlines menu. To overlay an exponential trendline on top of an already existing linear curve, simply click on the chart once, and click on the Trendlines menu. Figure 4.12 shows the linear and exponential trendlines for our example, with both equations shown. The equation for the exponential demand curve is given by

$$units\,sold = 28677 \times e^{-0.072 \times price}.$$

The formula to enter in the spreadsheet for year 2008 is therefore =MIN(28677*EXP(-0.072*$C$1), C7). This formula can then be copied to years 2009-2011.

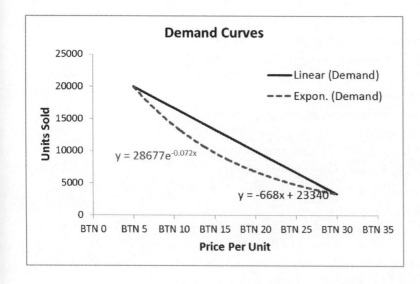

Figure 4.12: Linear and exponential demand curves for yoghurt project. The equations are used to integrate the demand curve information into the spreadsheet

Quadratic relationships are even more flexible, in that they allow U-shape relationships (also called "bathtub" curves) and inverse-U shapes. U-shape relationships are used for describing mortality rates as a function of age, where mortality rates are higher at infancy and old age, and lower in between. Similarly, they are used in capturing the reliability of systems over time, where failures are more likely to occur early or after wear-out begins. Creating a quadratic relationship that is nonlinear requires at least three {price, demand} pairs. In our example we would have to add a third set of values for price and demand in order to obtain a U-shape curve. Once the three points are specified, using trendlines follows the same steps as described for linear demand curves, by choosing a *polynomial* trendline with order 2. The formula for a quadratic function (or order-2 polynomial) is of the form:

$$y = a + bx + cx^2$$

where *a*,*b* and *c* are numbers. The resulting numeric formula is then integrated into the spreadsheet accordingly.

4.4   *Optimizing the outcome: Solver*

A different type of analysis, which is often useful when considering the effect of input factors on an outcome measure, is finding the combination of factor values that optimizes the outcome measure in some way, and under given conditions. In other words, we optimize an outcome measure, by varying one or more input factors, under some constraints.

The term *optimize* can mean maximizing, minimizing, or setting the outcome metric to a particular value. For example, in the yoghurt project an important question is how to price yoghurt cups. The Ministry of Agriculture might want to figure out which pricing maximizes NPV, given production costs and return rates in certain ranges.

Manual optimization can be achieved by entering many different combinations of the input factors, recording the resulting outcome measure, and determining which combination leads to the best outcome value. In our example, we would enter many different combinations of values for price, cost, and rate and find out which combination maximizes NPV. Such a manual solution quickly becomes tedious, as the number of input factors increases and the possible ranges of these factors widens. Moreover, manual entry of input values means that the user is considering only some, but not all, of the possible values. For example, I might consider 100 different cost values between 3-7 Nu. However, this range includes many more values, and in some cases a skipped value might be the one of interest. Hence, manual optimization is likely to give the wrong answer.

Excel has a powerful tool for optimizing an outcome metric of interest, called *Solver*. Given an optimization task, Solver searches all feasible input factor values and finds the combination that has the "best" outcome measure value (the largest value for maximum optimization, the smallest for minimum optimization). Such a combination is called an *optimal solution*. Some problems have no optimal solution, some have a unique solution, and others have multiple optimal solutions.

Installing Solver

Solver, which is an Excel add-in, comes with most installations of Microsoft Word. If it does not already appear in your *Data* > *Analysis* menu in Excel 2007 and 2010 (under the *Tools* menu in Excel 2003), install it by following these steps:

1. In *Files* choose *Options*

2. Click on *Add-Ins* (see Figure 4.13)

3. At the bottom choose *Manage Excel Add-Ins* and click *Go*

4. Check the Solver Add-in

Solver should now appear in your *Data* > *Analysis* menu.

Solver's Terminology

Solver requires three pieces of information: the input factors to modify, the outcome metric to optimize, and the constraints on any of the input factors or other factors in our spreadsheet. These three information bits have special terms in Solver:

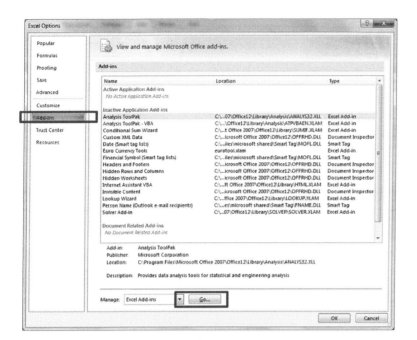

Figure 4.13: Installing Solver Add-in in Excel. In *File > Options* choose Add-Ins (top screenshot). Then check the Solver Add-in (bottom screenshot)

Variable cells are the cells on the spreadsheet with the input factor values that we want to vary. Solver does not allow these cells to contain formulas

Objective (Target) is the outcome metric to be optimized. Solver expects the Objective to be a function of the Changing cells (the input factors). The term *Target* is used in Excel 2007.

Constraints are restrictions on values in the variable cells

Example: Yoghurt Pricing

Let us consider the example of pricing yoghurt cups, such that NPV is optimized. We assume here that the price of a yoghurt cup is under our control. The *Objective* is NPV, located in cell C13. *Variable cells* is the price cell, located in C1. It might appear at first that charging the highest possible price would maximize NPV. However, recall that in the last section we linked demand to price via a demand curve function. Hence, increasing price also affects NPV indirectly by affecting the number of cups sold.

As for constraints, we require price to be no more than Nu 40 (due to marketing knowledge), but we also know that it must be a positive number (> 0). These constraints are written as[3]

$$price <= 40$$

and

$$price >= 0.$$

Finally, if we want to restrict monetary values to round ngultrum, we can include this in the constraints as the requirement that price should be an integer[4] This is written as

$$price\ Int.$$

After all the cells and constraints have been properly specified, we search for a solution. Placing the cursor in our spreadsheet and clicking Solver gives the Solver menu. Figure 4.14 shows how the *Objective*, *Variable Cells* and *Constraints* are entered for our example.

Next, click the *Solve* button. At this point Solver will search for the solution. In our case, the solution means the combination

[3] The sign $<=$ means that the left side is less than or equal to the right side. Here it means that price is less than or equal to 40. The sign $>=$ means that the left side is greater than or equal to the right side. Here it means that price is greater than or equal to 0.

[4] An integer is a number with no decimal points.

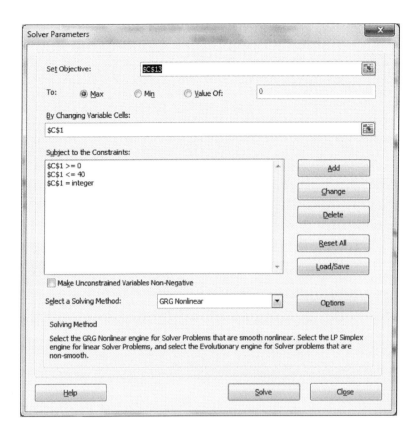

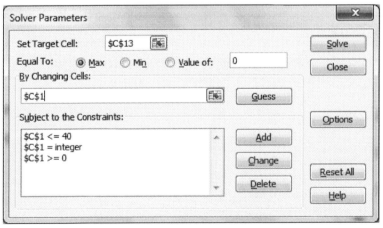

Figure 4.14: Inputting the NPV cell as Objective/Target cell, price as Variable Cells, and the various constraints. Top: Excel 2010. Bottom: Excel 2007

of price and cost that maximizes NPV. The next window tells us that "Solver found a solution" (see the bottom of the panel in Figure 4.15). In the same panel, we choose where to save solution. The default is "Keep Solver Solution", which means that the values in cells C1 and C13 will be replaced with the solution that Solver finds. Note that in this case, the numbers for *units sold* (line 9) also change, because of the relationship between price and demand. Solver also allows us to save this particular search under "Save Scenario". This is useful if we want to use the same setup again.

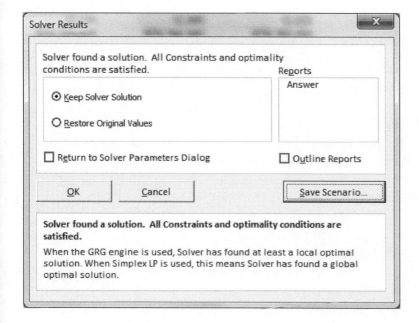

Figure 4.15: Solver found a solution for this example (see bottom of panel). The default will replace cells C1 and C14 with the solution

The solution obtained in our example is *price*=14, which yields the highest NPV among all possible pricing options between 0-40. Pricing below Nu 14 will drive NPV down by lowering revenues. Pricing above Nu 14 will drive down NPV by lowering demand. The maximum NPV value is reached at Nu 14 per cup, which yields an NPV of Nu 207,336.

	A	B	C	D	E	F
1		Price per unit	BTN 14			
2		Cost per unit	BTN 5			
3		Interest rate	4%			
4						
5			2008	2009	2010	2011
6		Year	1	2	3	4
7		Units produced	12,000	20,000	20,000	20,000
8		Total variable costs	BTN 60,000	BTN 100,000	BTN 100,000	BTN 100,000
9		Units sold	10,550	10,550	10,550	10,550
10		Revenues	BTN 146,523	BTN 146,523	BTN 146,523	BTN 146,523
11		Profit	BTN 86,523	BTN 46,523	BTN 46,523	BTN 46,523
12		Present value	BTN 83,195	BTN 43,013	BTN 41,359	BTN 39,768
13		Net Present Value	BTN 207,336			
14						
15						
16						
17		Units sold are a function of the Price per unit				
18						

Figure 4.16: The solution is found in cell C1: Price=14. This price leads to the highest NPV under the specified constraints (note that *units sold* numbers in line 9 also changed accordingly)

Further examples of Scenario building and optimization

To emphasize the wide range of projects where optimization is useful, we describe a few more examples where this a tool can improve planning.

Inventory Decisions: Consider a small restaurant serving fresh momos[5]. Momos are served by the plate, with five momos to a plate, all of the same type (cheese, beef, etc.). Every morning the owner prepares 200 plates. While 200 is a reasonable estimate for demand based on experience, there is less certainty about the types of momos that customers will order on any given day. The owner must therefore decide every morning how many of the 200 plates to prepare of each of three types: cheese, beef, and pork. Figure 4.17 presents a spreadsheet with the owner's information (unit=plate). At the top, we see the selling prices set by the owner (based on conventional pricing at other momo shops), and the cost per producing one plate, by type of momo. Below, information on amounts produced (determined by the owner) and amounts consumed is entered. For amounts produced, the owner makes sure that the total number of plates produced is 200 by setting the value for Pork (cell D7) to *200-B7-C7*.

One challenge is determining estimates for amounts consumed. While the owner is reasonably sure about the overall number of 200, he is uncertain about demand for each type of momo. Usually, at least 10 plates are consumed from each type.

[5] A momo is a Tibetan-style steamed dumpling that is a popular snack in Bhutan. Momos come with different fillings, including cheese, beef and pork.

Hence, he uses the function *randbetween(10,B7)* for generating a random number for cheese momo consumption in this range[6], and copies the formula for the beef and pork consumption cells. We discuss this approach for modeling uncertainty in detail in Chapter 6.

The next steps are straightforward: *Cost* is computed by multiplying the *Amount Produced* by *Unit Cost*. *Revenue* is computed by multiplying *Amount Consumed* by *Unit Sell Price*. And finally, Profit is computed by *Revenue − Cost*.

[6] A new random number will be generated each time you modify the spreadsheet. To generate a new random number directly, click the F9 key

	B8	fx	=RANDBETWEEN(10,B7)	
	A	B	C	D	E
1		Unit Sell price	Unit Cost		
2	Cheese Momo	35	10		
3	Beef Momo	45	15		
4	Pork Momo	45	15		
5					
6		Cheese	Beef	Pork	
7	Amount produced	53	51	88	
8	Consumed	46	30	34	
9	Cost	530	765	1320	
10	Revenue	1610	1350	1530	
11	Profit	1080	585	210	
12					
13	Daily Total Profit	1875			
14					

Figure 4.17: Spreadsheet setup for momo dilemma: how many to prepare of each type in order to maximize profit?

How does the daily profit change as the produced amounts of cheese, beef and pork momos change? This is where scenario building is useful. We can vary the number of cheese and beef momos produced in a two-way data table, and see the effect on the daily profit. Scenario building is also useful for tackling the uncertainty associated with the consumption of different types of momo: we can create a few scenarios such as "100 cheese, 50 beef, 50 pork" and "40 cheese, 100 beef, 60 pork" and evaluate daily profit based on such scenarios. This will give us not only an idea of the average daily profit, but also of how much this bottom line number can vary across different consumption patterns.

In this example, the owner could also use the data to determine what production breakdown maximizes daily profit. In other words, he can use Solver to find the optimal breakdown of the 200 daily momo plates into cheese, beef and pork. This is illustrated in Figure 4.18. We set the objective to the *Total Profit* value (cell B13), the *Changing Variable Cells* are B7, C7, D7, we constrain each of the amounts produced to be integers (no half plates!), and also make sure that we do not produce more than 100 plates of one particular kind on a certain day (for operational reasons).

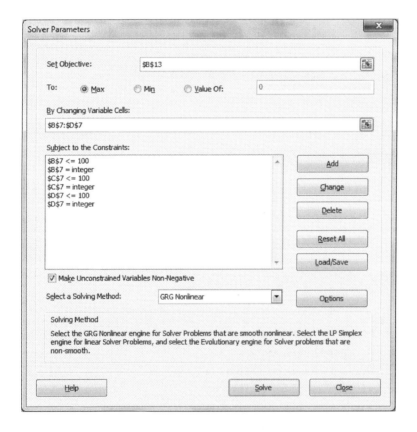

Figure 4.18: Setting up the momo preparation optimization problem in Solver

Solver found a solution: prepare 55 plates of cheese momo, 48 beef, and 93 pork (see Figure 4.19). This will give a maximum daily profit of Nu 3,565. Note, however, that the solution depends on the particular *Consumed* numbers, which are random numbers between 10 and the produced amounts. This extra level of uncertainty is not incorporated into the solution. In the next chapter, we will see the importance of capturing such uncertainty and how we can integrate it into our calculations.

	A	B	C	D
1		Unit Sell price	Unit Cost	
2	Cheese Momo	35	10	
3	Beef Momo	45	15	
4	Pork Momo	45	15	
5				
6		Cheese	Beef	Pork
7	Amount produced	55	48	93
8	Consumed	25	37	82
9	Cost	550	720	1395
10	Revenue	875	1665	3690
11	Profit	325	945	2295
12				
13	Daily Total Profit	3565		

Figure 4.19: Solver's solution

University Admissions: Several civil service organizations in Bhutan are in the process of becoming autonomous, among them the Royal University of Bhutan (RUB), which turned autonomous on July 1, 2011. Until then, only students who passed the university board exams were accepted by RUB, and tuition was free. Today, however, the new autonomous status of RUB has resulted in the need and ability to admit self-funding students. Goals of becoming autonomous have been stated as strengthening research and teaching capabilities. One decision that must be made is how many paying students to admit each year. For the first year, 177 seats were open to self-funding students, but it is yet to be decided how many seats to allocate in future. Various social, academic, and financial issues must be considered, for instance: will the more academically diverse classes pose challenges to the learning environment? Measuring success in terms of the project goal (enhanced research and teaching capabilities) must also include various aspects that are linked to the goal, and are important in themselves: academic achievements (average class performance and variability), career placement, faculty and student satisfaction, and achievement of relevant national goals.

Spreadsheets can be used for exploring the effects of self-funding admissions on outcomes of interest (academic and financial), using scenarios of interest.

Similar challenges arise regarding admission to private schools. With the growing demand for places at private schools in Bhutan, and especially in Thimphu, private schools must decide how much to expand. While increasing the student body provides an opportunity for a larger number of students to attend the school, classes that are too large pose challenges in terms of facilities, teachers, and attention to individual students. Once outcome measures are defined (academic, social, financial, and any other relevant metrics), admissions numbers can be placed in a spreadsheet to evaluate their potential impact on the outcomes.

Exercises

1. Create a column data table exploring the effect of *Rate of Return* on NPV, using the Rates: 4%, 6%, 8%, 10%.

2. Recreate the *Best Case* and *Worst Case* scenarios for the yoghurt project shown in Figure 4.5 using *Scenario Manager*. Then, add a third scenario called Medium Case, with values *price*=20 Nu, *cost*=5 Nu, *rate*=6%.

3. Recreate the exponential demand curve shown in Chapter 4. Use the resulting equation to replace the *units sold* cells in your spreadsheet with an appropriate formula.

4. Using the spreadsheet with the exponential demand formula for *units sold*, find the price that maximizes NPV.

5. Assume that the Ministry of Agriculture only wants to meet a required NPV of Nu 150,000. What is the lowest price of a yoghurt cup that achieves this NPV?

6. Create a one-way data table exploring the effect of price on NPV, using the spreadsheet with the exponential demand curve formula. Use steps of Nu 1 between 0-40 for price. Plot the resulting relationship using a scatter plot.

5 *Measuring Performance and Risk*

RECALL THE YOGHURT PROJECT example, where we computed
NPV under different scenarios. Figure 5.1 displays the NPV
of the project under three scenarios: best case, worst case, and
medium case. In the best case, we sell at high prices, produce
at low cost, and the return rate is low. The opposite is true for
the worst case, and the medium case lies somewhere between
the two. Looking at the numbers, should the Ministry of Agriculture invest in this project? If your answer is "yes", then you
are likely focusing on the best case NPV (Nu 609,453) or even
the medium case (Nu 217,949). If you think "no", then you might
be focusing on the worst case scenario (NPV= Nu -133,389). The
real question is: which scenario will eventually materialize?

Scenario	Best Case	Worst Case	Medium Case
Price	BTN 30	BTN 10	BTN 20
Cost	BTN 5	BTN 7	BTN 6
Interest Rate	4%	8%	6%
NPV	BTN 609,453	-BTN 133,389	BTN 217,949

Figure 5.1: Three scenarios
of yoghurt project with their
projected NPVs

In discussing scenarios, we pinpointed one important source
of uncertainty in project planning: the future. Because we do
not know which scenario will eventually materialize, we look
at various possibilities. The next step is to quantify the uncertainty by attaching probabilities to the different scenarios. For
example, consider the following probabilities for each of the
three scenarios: 40% chance of the best case, 30% chance of the
worst case, and 30% chance of the medium case scenarios (per-
centages must add up to 100%). Now, should the Ministry of

Agriculture invest in this project? In this chapter we will look at measures of performance and risk that take into account the uncertainty regarding which scenario will materialize. We will look at two important and popular measures: average (expected) performance, and volatility (risk).

5.1   Expected performance

A common way to evaluate the outcome of a project across possible scenarios is to take an average. In particular, we take a weighted average, such that each scenario has a weight equal to its probability of occurrence. More probable scenarios will thus have a larger weight in the average. The average performance is also called *Expected Performance*. In the yoghurt project example, with the scenario probabilities given in Figure 5.2, we compute the Expected Performance in terms of NPV (the *expected NPV* in this case) as

$$
\begin{aligned}
\text{Expected NPV} \quad = \quad & \text{NPV(Best Case)} \times \text{Prob(Best Case)} \qquad\qquad (5.1)\\
+ \quad & \text{NPV(Worst Case)} \times \text{Prob(Worst Case)}\\
+ \quad & \text{NPV(Medium Case)} \times \text{Prob(Medium Case)}\\
= \quad & 0.4 \times 609,453 + 0.3 \times (-133,389) + 0.3 \times 217.949 = 269,149
\end{aligned}
$$

Scenario	Best Case	Worst Case	Medium Case
Price	BTN 30	BTN 10	BTN 20
Cost	BTN 5	BTN 7	BTN 6
Interest Rate	4%	8%	6%
NPV	BTN 609,453	-BTN 133,389	BTN 217,949
Probability	0.4	0.3	0.3

Figure 5.2: Three scenarios of yoghurt project with their projected NPVs and scenario probabilities

The expected performance, which is a weighted average, can be considered an estimate of long-term performance. This is useful in cases when the event of interest is repeated multiple times, and the average performance is of interest. For example, the average time it takes us to get to work each morning is meaningful because we repeat the same path every day, even though the actual time to work varies from day to day (due to traffic and other uncontrollable factors).

Computing the *Expected Performance* in Excel can be done using multiplication and addition (=B6*B7+C6*C7+D6*D7), or more simply, using the function =*sumproduct(NPV cells,Probability cells)*, as shown in Figure 5.3. The three NPV values are in cells B6:D6, and the corresponding probabilities are in cells B7:D7. The function *sumproduct(B6:D6,B7:D7)* multiplies each of the NPV values by its corresponding probability, and then sums up the three multiplied numbers. Using the *sumproduct* function is less error-prone than multiplication and addition, especially as the number of scenarios increases.

	B10	▼	f_x	=SUMPRODUCT(B6:D6,B7:D7)	
	A	B	C	D	E
1	Scenario	Best Case	Worst Case	Medium Case	
2	Price	BTN 30	BTN 10	BTN 20	
3	Cost	BTN 5	BTN 7	BTN 6	
4	Interest Rate	4%	8%	6%	
5					
6	NPV	BTN 609,453	-BTN 133,389	BTN 217,949	
7	Probability	0.4	0.3	0.3	
8					
9					
10	Expected NPV	269,149			

Figure 5.3: Computing expected NPV using the function *SUMPRODUCT*

The expected performance is affected not only by the values of the outcome measure (NPV in our example), but also by the probabilities of the different scenarios materialising. Changing the probabilities can drastically affect the expected performance. In our example, the difference between best and worst case scenarios is substantial, and therefore changing the probability of the worst and/or best case scenario can greatly affect the expected NPV.

Interpreting Expected Performance

Computing the expected performance of a project is useful for two main purposes. First, it allows us to gauge the level of the expected outcome measure across a range of possible scenarios. Having such a number in hand can help us carry out more informed decisions. Second, the expected performance number is useful for comparing the performance of different projects. While we have discussed a single project in isolation thus far, in reality we often consider multiple avenues for investing resources. In such cases, it is important to be able to compare the projected results of the different projects under different scenarios.

Let us consider an alternative to the yoghurt plant project. Suppose that the Ministry of Agriculture is debating between the production and sale of yoghurt and of ice cream. Both projects share the goals of promoting local dairy industries, providing employment, and promoting health benefits from introducing more milk into the local diet. Suppose that the same facility (with appropriate machinery) and the same manpower (with proper training) would be used in either project. Consider the three scenarios for the ice cream project in Figure 5.4. We consider the same three input factors: price, cost, and return rate. We then consider *best case*, *worst case*, and *medium case*, similar to the yoghurt project. The two differences between the projects are production costs (producing an ice cream cup ranges between Nu 3-5) and pricing (an ice cream cup is priced in the range Nu 10-20). The rate of return is obviously the same for both projects. In addition, the probabilities of the three scenarios are identical to those of the yoghurt project, because both projects rely on the same resources and environments.

Comparing the two projects, we see that the expected performance of the ice cream project, in terms of expected NPV, is Nu 224,761, which is lower than the yoghurt project expected NPV by approximately Nu 45,000 (see Figure 5.3). What does this comparison tell us about the two projects? It tells us that, taking into account the different scenarios and their probabilities of occurrence, the yoghurt project is expected to yield an NPV that is higher by an average of Nu 45,000. Whether this difference is meaningful or not depends on the context. Nu 45,000 can be a very large amount in some cases but an insignificant amount in a million-dollar project. Obviously, evaluating the outcome of a

B10		fx	=SUMPRODUCT(B6:D6,B7:D7)	
	A	B	C	D	E

	A	B	C	D	E
1	Scenario	Best Case	Worst Case	Medium Case	
2	Price	BTN 20	BTN 10	BTN 15	
3	Cost	BTN 3	BTN 5	BTN 4	
4	Interest Rate	4%	8%	6%	
5					
6	NPV	BTN 427,937	-BTN 15,719	BTN 194,339	
7	Probability	0.4	0.3	0.3	
8					
9					
10	Expected NPV	224,761			

Figure 5.4: Three scenarios and expected NPV for ice cream project

project should not be measured by a single metric (such as NPV). In our example we might also consider health benefits, employment, development of local industries (as a national goal), and effects on local culture and society.

Setting Probabilities

You might wonder how the probabilities for the three scenarios were obtained, or more generally, how do we assign a probability to a scenario? In most cases these probabilities are based on subjective information and expertise. How likely is the best scenario to occur in our example? That depends on the chances of the rate of return being low in the next 4 years, on production costs being low during that period, and on high pricing. Only the latter is under our direct control, and hence we must use financial, operational and other expertise and domain knowledge to devise scenario probabilities. It is therefore useful to use the collective expertise from the various departments of an organization (finance, marketing, sales, operations, etc.)

While the inclusion of subjective probabilities in itself introduces another layer of uncertainty into our computations, the good news is that we can use the same approach to evaluate the effect of this uncertainty on our numbers of interest. In particular, we can modify the probabilities and see how they affect the expected performance. This can be done using one-way and two-way data tables or even the *Scenario Manager*. If we have only two scenarios, then a one-way data table is sufficient for modifying the probability of the first scenario (since the probabilities of the two scenarios must add up to 1, the probability of the second scenario is automatically given once the first scenario probability is chosen). For three scenarios, a two-way data table allows modifying each of the probabilities of scenarios one and two (the third scenario probability is automatically given once the other two are chosen). For more than three scenarios, where we want to modify more than two probabilities, we can use *Scenario Manager*.

5.2   Volatility and risk

When comparing the yoghurt and ice cream projects in terms of expected NPV we asked what can be learned from comparing the expected performance numbers. We now ask what *cannot* be learned by such numbers. Consider again the two projects under each of the three scenarios (best case, worst case, medium case). Which project would you advise the Ministry of Agriculture to implement, even if we consider NPV as the single outcome measure of interest?

Although the yoghurt project has a higher expected NPV than the ice cream project, note that under the worst case scenario the ice cream project incurs a much lower loss. We also see that in the best case scenario, the yoghurt project is expected to be much more successful. In other words, the NPV of the yoghurt project appears to be more variable across the three scenarios. We can say that the yoghurt project NPV is more volatile, or risky. While expected performance gives an indication of average performance across all scenarios of interest, it does not tell us about how volatile performance can be across the scenarios. Expected performance does not tell us about risk.

In many cases, a project is implemented on a one time basis, and we will only see the outcome under a single scenario. It is therefore informative to know how risky a project is and how "wildly" might the outcome vary across scenarios. We can assess risk by examining the NPV values under the three scenarios for the yoghurt project and compare them to the corresponding numbers for the ice cream project. Figure 5.5 compares the two projects by graphically presenting their NPVs for the different scenarios. We see that the ice cream NPV values vary less than than those for the yoghurt project.

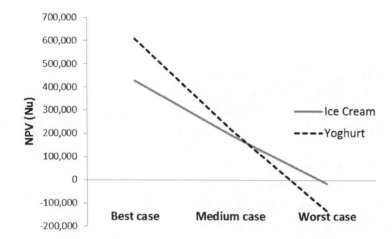

Figure 5.5: Comparison of NPV of yoghurt and ice cream projects across the three scenarios. NPV varies less across scenarios for the ice cream project

However, if we have more scenarios or more projects, such comparisons can become complicated. A popular approach is therefore to use a single measure of volatility or risk called the *standard deviation*. The standard deviation measures how scattered the outcome values are across the different scenarios. More accurately, it measures how scattered the outcome values are across the expected performance. In low risk projects, we expect NPV values to be close to the expected NPV (indicating that NPV does not vary much across scenarios). In high risk projects, NPV values will greatly vary from the expected NPV.

The standard deviation measure of risk is based on computing the deviation of each NPV from the expected NPV. In particular, it sums all the squared deviations of NPV values from the expected NPV. The computation follows four steps:

1. For each scenario (i), compute the difference (deviation) between the NPV and the expected NPV: $d_i = NPV_i - ENPV$

2. Square each of the deviations: $d_i^2 = (NPV_i - ENPV)^2$

3. Take a weighted average of the squared deviations, using the probabilities as weights: $\sum_i d_i^2 \times Prob_i$. This is called the *variance*.

4. Take a square root of the variance. You now have the *standard deviation*.

Let us illustrate this computation using Excel. We use the spreadsheet that has the three scenarios with NPV and expected NPV numbers for the yoghurt project (Figure 5.3). The NPV numbers are in cells B6:D6 and the expected NPV is in cell B10. We add a new row (row 8) with squared deviations, computed using the formula *=(B6-$B$10)^2* for *best case*, and then copy the formula to the other scenarios. The resulting numbers are very large (see Figure 5.6). Then, we take a weighted average of the squared deviations, by multiplying each by its corresponding probability, and finally we take a square root. These steps can be done with a single formula: *=sqrt(sumproduct(B8:D8,B7:D7))*, as shown in Figure 5.6.

Interpreting Standard Deviations

For the yoghurt project we obtain a standard deviation of NPV equal to Nu 309,387. Note that the units of the standard deviation are identical to those of the original metric (in our example, the NPV units are in Nu). This is because we took a square root in the last step of the computation, thereby reversing the effect of squaring the numbers in the first step.

Standard deviations alone are not necessarily useful for evaluating risk. However, they are very useful in comparing risk across different projects. For example, the bottom of Figure 5.6 shows the standard deviation for the ice cream project[1] which is equal to Nu 184,768. As expected, the standard deviation of the ice cream project NPV is much lower than that of the yoghurt project NPV, indicating lower risk.

[1] The ice cream NPV standard deviation can easily be obtained by replacing the NPV numbers in the yoghurt spreadsheet

B12		f_x	=SQRT(SUMPRODUCT(B8:D8,B7:D7))	
	A	B	C	D	E

	A	B	C	D	E
1	Scenario	Best Case	Worst Case	Medium Case	
2	Price	BTN 30	BTN 10	BTN 20	
3	Cost	BTN 5	BTN 7	BTN 6	
4	Interest Rate	4%	8%	6%	
5					
6	NPV	BTN 609,453	-BTN 133,389	BTN 217,949	
7	Probability	0.4	0.3	0.3	
8	Squared Deviations	1.15807E+11	1.62037E+11	2621484362	
9					
10	Expected NPV	269,149			
11					
12	standard deviation	309,387			
13					

B8		f_x	=(B6-$B$10)^2	

	A	B	C	D
1	Scenario	Best Case	Worst Case	Medium Case
2	Price	BTN 20	BTN 10	BTN 15
3	Cost	BTN 3	BTN 5	BTN 4
4	Interest Rate	4%	8%	6%
5				
6	NPV	BTN 427,937	-BTN 15,719	BTN 194,339
7	Probability	0.4	0.3	0.3
8	Squared Deviations	4.1281E+10	5.7831E+10	925494802
9				
10	Expected NPV	224,761		
11				
12	standard deviation	184,768		
13				

Figure 5.6: Computing the standard deviation of NPV for the yoghurt project (top) and the ice cream project (bottom)

5.3 Comparing projects

As mentioned earlier, in real life, the choice of whether to invest in a project or not typically comes with alternative projects or investment options. We therefore must decide not *whether* to invest in a certain project but rather *in which* project to invest (including the option of investing the money in non-project alternatives).

The two performance measures that were described earlier, *expected performance* and *standard deviation*, can be used to compare projects in terms of their expected outcome (averaged across different scenarios) and their risk. In our example, the yoghurt project indicated higher expected performance compared to the ice cream alternative, but also higher risk. Such behavior is typical of investments: higher risk is often accompanied by higher average gain. Otherwise, high-risk investments would not be attractive at all!

Choosing to invest in one project over alternatives is relevant when the execution of one project precludes other projects from being undertaken. Yet, in some cases it is possible to execute multiple projects simultaneously. In the next chapter we look at the possibility of combining projects.

Exercises

1. Create a spreadsheet for the ice cream project, similar to the yoghurt spreadsheet in Figure 3.7. Compared to the yoghurt spreadsheet, modify only the values for *price per unit*, *cost per unit*, and *interest rate*.

2. Using Scenario Manager, create three scenarios for the ice cream project, as shown in Figure 5.4.

3. Add probabilities to the three scenarios, as shown in Figure 5.4, and compute the expected NPV using the *sumproduct* function.

4. Modify the scenario probabilities so that the best case has a probability of 0.6 and the worst case has a probability of 0.1. What should be the probability of the medium case scenario?

5. What is the *expected NPV* under the new set of probabilities? Why did the expected performance increase/decrease compared to the previous set of probabilities?

6. Comparing the yoghurt and ice cream projects, find a set of scenario probabilities (Prob(Best Case), Prob(Worst Case), Prob(Medium Case)) that make the ice cream project more attractive in terms of higher expected NPV. Assume that both projects share the same set of scenario probabilities.

7. Using the original scenario probabilities of 0.4,0.3,0.3, compute the standard deviation of NPV for the ice cream project. The bottom of Figure 5.6 shows the ice cream spreadsheet with squared deviations (note the function used in cell B8), and the resulting standard deviation.

8. Modify the scenario probabilities so that the best case has a probability of 0.6 and the worst case has a probability of 0.1. What is the resulting standard deviation?

9. Comparing the yoghurt and ice cream projects, find a set of scenario probabilities (Prob(Best Case), Prob(Worst Case), Prob(Medium Case)) which make the ice cream project more attractive in terms of lower risk (smaller standard deviation).

We shall assume that both projects share the same set of scenario probabilities.

10. Using the probabilities in (9), compare the expected performance of the two projects. Which is a better investment? Explain.

6   *Incorporating Randomness via Simulation*

THE DIFFERENT METHODS DESCRIBED THUS FAR are aimed at capturing as much information as possible from available numbers related to projects of interest. The project planning context consists of generating projections into the future in order to make informative decisions in the present. The methods that we looked at aim not only at capturing the relationship between input factors and outcome metrics of interest, but also at assessing the level of uncertainty associated with this relationship. For example, we looked at ranges of input factors (price range, cost range, rate of return range) and evaluated the outcome of interest (NPV) as the input factors varied within these ranges. We used Excel's data tables and Scenario Manager for this purpose. Solver was used to find a combination of input factors that optimizes an outcome measurement of interest.

We also used probabilities to incorporate the uncertainty associated with the different scenarios. We then computed measures of expected performance and risk that take into account the scenario probabilities.

In short, our two approaches to uncertainty thus far focused on specifying reasonable ranges for uncertain numbers, and assigning probabilities to uncertain events. We now further expand our toolkit for assessing the outcome measure under uncertainty in the input factors. This is done by incorporating randomness into the input factors and evaluating the outcome under this added randomness. This approach is called *simulation*, and in particular, *Monte Carlo simulation*. With simulation we can answer questions regarding the outcome measure of interest such as: What is the probability that the NPV will be negative? What is the probability that the daily profit will be above Nu 3000? What is the probability that the project will be completed within a year? What is the probability that hospital admissions will decrease?

While creating scenarios is one type of simulation, *Monte Carlo simulation* refers to a different type of simulation, where we convey uncertainty in terms of probabilities and then generate event outcomes according to those probabilities. By simulating the event outcomes many times, we assess how the outcome metrics of interest behave across different scenarios, and how much uncertainty to expect.

Here is a simple example: Given the three scenarios for the yoghurt project (best case, medium case, worst case) and the probabilities that we assigned to them (0.4, 0.3, 0.3), Monte Carlo simulation can be used to repeatedly simulate scenario materialization according to these probabilities. Since the event outcome is simulated many times (say, 1,000 times), we expect approximately 40% of the simulations to generate "best case", 30% "medium case", and 30% "worst case".

We touched upon the simulation approach in Chapter 4 (Section 4.3), when studying the breakdown of momo types to be prepared each day by the shop owner. At the start of each day, we know the overall daily demand but we do not know the demand for each type of momo plate (recall that while the momo shop owner is reasonably sure about the overall number of 200 plates, he is uncertain about demand for each type of momo, and usually at least 10 plates are consumed from each type). This statement gives us the following numbers as well as levels of confidence in these numbers:

- The estimated overall daily demand is 200 plates, and the owner is highly confident about this number.

- The estimated daily demand for a particular momo type is somewhere between 10 plates and the amount produced, with no particular value being more likely than another.

We conveyed the first piece of information by using the value 200 with no range of uncertainty around it. The second piece was conveyed by the function =*randbetween(10,B7)* for plates of cheese momos, =*randbetween(10,C7)* for beef and =*randbetween(10,D7)* for pork [1]. In other words, we *simulated* the daily demand for each momo type. The advantage of simulation is that we can simulate new values over and over again in order to see how different values affect our calculations, and most importantly, our decisions. Let us now examine simulation in a more methodical way.

[1] B7, C7 and D7 are the cells with the amount produced of cheese, beef, and pork momo plates, respectively

6.1   Functions for generating random numbers

Excel has a range of functions that support generating random numbers. The functions differ in the types of numbers generated and in the probability of generating the different values. We focus here on two useful functions: *randbetween* and *rand*.

The function =*randbetween(a,b)* generates a random integer between two numbers *a* and *b*. For example, *randbetween(2,5)* generates a random integer between 2 and 5. All integers in the range $[a, b]$ are equally likely to be generated, and therefore this function is useful when we know the feasible range of a measurement, but are *completely uncertain* about where the value will fall within that range. This would be the case if we were rolling a die, which can fall on 1,2,3,4,5,6 with equal chance. In the momo example, we used *randbetween* because the number of plates consumed is an integer (we do not consider half plates).

The function =*rand()* generates a random number between 0 and 1. When we are completely uncertain about a probability of some event, we could use *rand* to generate a random probability. The *rand* function can also be used to generate a random number between any two numbers *a* and *b* by typing =*a+(b-a)*rand()*. For example, to generate a random return rate between 4% and 7.5% we use =*4+(7.5-4)*rand()* or simply =*4+3.5*rand()*. To generate a new random number, press the F9 key. A new number will also be generated any time a change is made to the Excel spreadsheet.

6.2   *Regenerating random numbers and collecting them*

The strength of simulation is the ability to examine an outcome
of interest over a large range of simulated input factors. Functions such as *rand* and *randbetween* yield a single random number. We can regenerate new numbers by pressing F9 or by simply
modifying the worksheet. But how can we examine the results
under many different randomly generated values? For instance,
in our momo project example, how does the total daily profit
vary with different values for the simulated demand numbers?

One useful tool for accumulating the results from multiple
random number generations is Excel's data tables. We follow the
same steps as described in Section 4.1 for building a data table
but with a twist: in a one-way column table the "column input
cell" is left blank! This will generate a table with as many re-
generations of random numbers as we like, and for each random
number the table will give the outcome measurement of interest.
To illustrate this, consider the momo example where we want
to study how the daily total profit varies as the consumption
numbers of cheese, beef and pork momos vary according to
the *randbetween* function. Let's say that we want to generate
1,000 different random numbers. To do this, we create a one-way
column data table with two columns. The first column includes
index numbers 1,2,3,...,1000. The second column will include the
total daily profit for each random number generation. To easily
create a column with index numbers from 1 to 1,000 in Excel,
type "1" in the first cell, then use the Series dialog box (*Home>
Editing > Series*) as shown in Figure 6.1.

The spreadsheet with the setup for this type of one-way data
table and the resulting table are shown in Figure 6.2. Note that
recreating this table will generate different numbers in column
G, because of the random number generation. We see that some
of the daily profit numbers are negative! We can compute different statistics such as the average, minimum and maximum
of Column G to get a feel of the total daily profit distribution
(remember to exclude the value in cell G2).

Moreover, we can answer questions such as What is the probability that the daily profit will be below Nu 3,000? To do this,

Figure 6.1: Creating a column with index numbers in Excel 2010, using the Fill Series dialog box

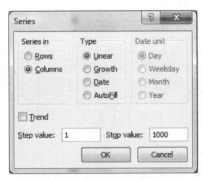

we compute the proportion of the 1,000 values that are below Nu 3,000. We can use Excel's formula *countif* to return the number of values below (or above) a certain profit value, and then divide it by the number of simulations. In this example, *=countif(G3:G1002,"<3000") / 1000* would yield the wanted probability. The function *percentrank* is efficient for finding what proportion of values are below a given number. In our example, we would use *=percentrank(G3:G1002,3000)*. The result would be identical to the *countif* result. The advantage of *percentrank* over *countif* is that the user does not need to specify the number of simulations.

Charts such as histograms[2] help convey the "big picture", as illustrated in Figure 6.3. We can see that the great majority of the daily profit values are positive, ranging mostly between approximately Nu 200-4,000.

[2] Creating a histogram in Excel is explained on the author's blog at www.bzst.com/2009/06/ histograms-in-excel.html

Two-way tables for two sources of uncertainty

The use of data tables for integrating simulated (that is, randomly generated) values can be further extended to include randomness in an input factor of interest. For example, in the momo spreadsheet shown in Figure 6.2, the owner produces 55 cheese, 48 beef and 97 pork momo plates. Suppose the owner wants to

	RAND	▾	× ✓ fx	=B13			
	A	B	C	D	E	F	G
1		Unit Sell price	Unit Cost			Simulation	Daily Total Profit
2	Cheese Momo	35	10				=B13
3	Beef Momo	45	15			1	
4	Pork Momo	45	15			2	
5						3	
6		Cheese	Beef	Pork		4	
7	Amount produced	55	48	97		5	
8	Consumed	52	38	64		6	
9	Cost	550	720	1455		7	
10	Revenue	1820	1710	2880		8	
11	Profit	1270	990	1425		9	
12						10	
13	Daily Total Profit	3685				11	
14						12	
15						13	
16						14	
17						15	
18						16	
19						17	
20						18	
21						19	
22						20	
23						21	
24						22	
25						23	

F	G
Simulation	Daily Total Profit
	4095
1	600
2	-230
3	30
4	4215
5	1185
6	985
7	1020
8	955
9	1680
10	3185
11	1295
12	2675
13	345
14	1410
15	4865
16	1335
17	3610
18	4415
19	320
20	2360
21	2950
22	785
23	2845

Figure 6.2: Left: Setting up a spreadsheet for a one-way column table (columns F-G) that computes total daily profit for different random number generations of the consumed amounts in cells B7:D7. Right: Resulting table.

explore the effect of different ratios of vegetarian (cheese) to non-vegetarian (beef and pork) momos. Note that the price and cost of beef and pork momos are identical, so we can group them into "non-veg". The owner considers three ratios: 50/150, 100/100, and 150/50. We can use a two-way data table to explore these options, where the rows correspond to the three ratios and the columns correspond to the 1,000 simulations. This is shown in Figure 6.4.

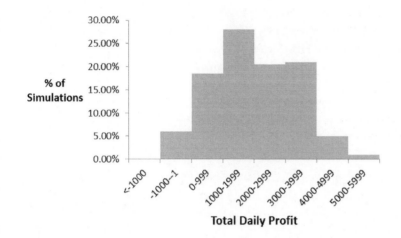

Figure 6.3: Distribution of daily total profit based on the 1,000 simulated values. The histogram shows the % of simulated values in each range of total profit numbers

We display the results from comparing the three veg/non-veg production ratios using histograms in Figure 6.5. It appears as though the 150/50 ratio produces the highest average profit, but note that it also has the smallest chance of falling in the highest profit range (Nu 4,500-5,000). We can also compare the probability of daily profit being above some desirable value across the three scenarios (using the *percentrank* function). Finally, it is useful to regenerate the data a few more times and examine the chart, to make sure that the main patterns are insensitive to the specific random numbers.

Exercises

Recall the example from Chapter 3 (Exercise #1):

A 2005 article in the Kuensel newspaper entitled *'Egg-cellent'* *business*[3] describes the following business supplying local eggs:

[3] The article is available on-line at kuenselonline.com/ 2010/modules.php?name= News&file=article&sid= 5853

> "The Satara farm in Langjophakha supplies about 40 cartons (8,400) of local eggs a week to numerous grocery stores in Thimphu. Established in 2000 with 250 birds, the farm today has about 500 birds and earns more than Nu 700 a day.

> According to proprietor Drimi Wangda, they collect about 400 eggs each day and a tray of 30 eggs is sold for Nu 130.

> While the business was profitable, it required hard work according to Drimi Wangda. "The birds are delicate creatures and their maintenance and the feeds need extra attention," he said.

> The birds are given de-worming tablets every two months and vaccinated once in three months. "The chicken feed is the most expensive," he said. "A kilogramme costs Nu. 13 and more than 700 kilogrammes is required in a month."

Using the spreadsheet for computing a 3-year NPV from Chapter 1, let us introduce some reasonable randomness into the input factors.

1. Assume that the number of eggs per day varies randomly in the range 350-450 eggs (should you use *rand* or *randbetween*?). Create a one-way column data table with 500 simulations of the NPV.

2. Using the one-way data table that you created, compute the probability that the NPV will exceed Nu 1,000,000. Remember that this is the proportion of values among the 500 simulations that exceed 1,000,000.

3. Press F9 to refresh the simulations. Report the probability that the NPV will exceed Nu 1,000,000. Did it change drastically from the previous number?

4. Now, add more randomness by including the fluctuating market price of eggs. Vary the sales price of an egg randomly between Nu 3-7, allowing all values in this range (including, for instance, Nu 4.35).

F1 | fx =B13

	A	B	C	D	E	F	G	H	I	J
1		Unit Sell price	Unit Cost			4075	50	100	150	
2	Cheese Momo	35	10			1				
3	Non-Veg Momo	45	15			2				
4						3				
5						4				
6		Cheese	Non-veg			5				
7	Amount produced	50	150			6				
8	Consumed	15	140			7				
9	Cost	500	2250			8				
10	Revenue	525	6300			9				
11	Profit	25	4050			10				
12						11				
13	Daily Total Profit	4075				12				
14						13				
15						14				
16						15				
17						16				
18						17				
19						18				
20						19				
21						20				
22						21				
23						22				
24						23				
25						24				
26						25				

Data Table

Row input cell: $B$7
Column input cell: $A$15

OK   Cancel

F	G	H	I
3940	50	100	150
1	2445	2130	2890
2	5370	740	750
3	4595	2345	680
4	1035	615	4370
5	1930	10	1785
6	3075	3320	1435
7	760	2405	3210
8	-10	2425	305
9	1595	3275	1850
10	4935	2330	3435
11	1485	4170	1540
12	5075	3125	1365
13	1535	1830	4155
14	5030	2280	4000
15	3290	4255	2235
16	1295	-235	1220
17	765	625	2760
18	3045	-315	3230
19	4530	2770	3880
20	1050	5185	5020
21	50	3635	1160
22	1485	2725	-370
23	-35	490	420
24	1980	1840	1035
25	2145	750	3280

Figure 6.4: Left: Setting up a spreadsheet for a two-way table (columns F-I) that computes total daily profit for multiple simulations of the consumed amounts of veg and non-veg momos (in cells B7:C7), for three different amounts of produced veg momo (modifying cell B7). The blank column cell $A$15 is used to generate the random numbers. Right: Resulting table with multiple simulations (in rows), and different amounts of cheese momo production (in columns). Recreating this table will generate different numbers in columns G-I

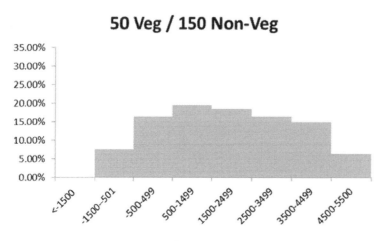

Figure 6.5: Comparing distributions of total daily profit for three different veg/non-veg momo production ratios, each based on 1,000 simulated values. The histograms show the % of simulated values in each range of total profit numbers

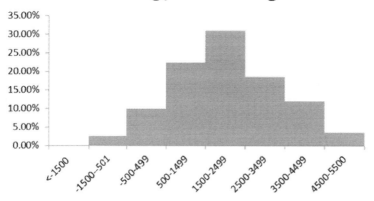

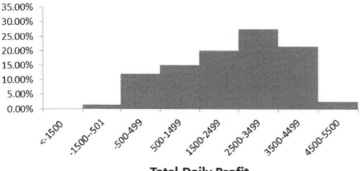

7   *Risk Reduction via Project Portfolios*

7.1   *Combining projects*

A WINNING STRATEGY IN FINANCIAL INVESTMENTS is the idea of diversification, or *portfolios*. A financial portfolio is a group of investments (e.g., in different stocks and bonds) that together constitute and are managed as one entity. Investing in a portfolio compared to a single asset is a strategy for reducing risk. The same idea exists for project portfolios. The only difference is that in the context of projects, portfolios make sense only when it is logistically and logically feasible to combine projects, given the constraints of each project.

To determine whether a set of projects can be combined, we must consider the nature of the different projects as well as the investor's objectives and constraints. On the one hand, it makes sense to group projects that support or enable other projects. An infrastructure project to lay fiber-optic cables to a certain area can enhance projects that rely on broadband availability in the same area, such as distance learning. On the other hand, we would not group projects that are contradictory or that try to achieve the same objective in different ways (for example, implementing two different reading-enhancement programs at all primary schools at the same time). In term of the investor, the choice of projects to include in the portfolio must take into account the ability of the investor to manage all of its components. For instance, a school or university might not be able to simultaneously upgrade its physical facilities, revise its academic curriculum, and expand its extra-curricular activities.

Let us consider the hypothetical Ministry of Agriculture's yoghurt and ice cream projects. Suppose the ministry's goals are to support and develop the local dairy industry, to provide jobs for youth, and to introduce local calcium-rich foods into citizens' diets. Suppose that the investment must be financially viable, such that the 4-year NPV is at least Nu 220,000. Assume also that it is logistically possible to carry out both projects, using the same materials and resources. Given these objectives and constraints, the yoghurt and ice cream projects can be combined into a portfolio. The question is whether this portfolio will outperform each of the individual projects.

In the following, we assume that it is possible to invest in and implement a combination of the projects under consideration. We will try to answer the following questions:

1. How to evaluate the performance of a portfolio of projects?

2. How does diversification reduce risk?

3. How to choose the right combination of projects?

7.2   Evaluating the performance of a portfolio

To assess the performance of a portfolio over individual projects, we can compute the same two performance measures of expected performance and standard deviation of the portfolio.

Let us consider combining the yoghurt and ice cream projects. As mentioned earlier, we assume that the same facility and resources are used two days a week to produce yoghurt and four days a week to produce ice cream. The sales counter then sells both items. The portfolio of projects therefore combines 1/3 "yoghurt" plus 2/3 "ice cream". How does this portfolio perform? We must evaluate it by measuring the different outcome metrics defined by the Ministry of Agriculture. For simplicity, we focus on NPV computations. However, the same logic applies to any other metric of interest.

Portfolio Expected Performance

Computing the expected NPV of the portfolio is straightforward, since we can assume that investing a fraction p of the total investment amount results in $p \times NPV$. For example, if we invest half the amount in the yoghurt project, then the resulting expected NPV would be half the amount expected under 100% investment in the yoghurt project.

In our example, the portfolio invests 1/3 in yoghurt and 2/3 in ice cream. Hence, the expected NPV of the portfolio is qual to one third of the yoghurt project expected NPV (Nu 269,149) plus two thirds of the ice cream project expected NPV (Nu 224,761):

$$
\begin{aligned}
\text{Portfolio expected NPV} \ &= \ 1/3 \times \text{yoghurt expected NPV} \\
&+ \ 2/3 \times \text{ice cream expected NPV} \\
&= \ 1/3 \times 269,149 + 2/3 \times 224,761 \\
&= \ Nu \ 239,557
\end{aligned}
$$

We see that the expected performance of the portfolio is somewhere between that of each of the two individual projects. We can affect how close this expected performance is to a given project by modifying the weights 1/3 and 2/3 (which must add up to 1). Figure 7.1 shows the expected performance of the portfolio as we change the ratio of yoghurt to ice cream production. The left side of the plot shows the extreme case of producing only ice cream (that is, executing only the ice cream project), and the right side shows the extreme case of producing only yoghurt (executing only the yoghurt project). Obviously, the more yoghurt produced, the higher the expected NPV.

If the portfolio achieves lower expected performance compared to the "best" project, then what is the advantage of a portfolio? We will see next that the advantage is in terms of risk reduction, as measured by the standard deviation.

7.3   Portfolio risk

The expected performance of a portfolio is easily computed from the expected performance of the individual projects' expected performance measures. We showed that the expected NPV of the

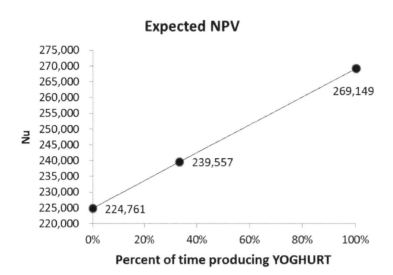

Expected NPV

269,149

239,557

224,761

Nu

Percent of time producing YOGHURT

Figure 7.1: Expected NPV for different combinations of the yoghurt and ice cream projects. The extreme points correspond to producing only ice cream (left) and only yoghurt (right). The point in the middle corresponds to producing yoghurt 2 days per week (33% of the time) and ice cream 4 days per week

portfolio is easy to compute from the expected NPV of the individual projects. However, computing the standard deviation of a portfolio, which is a measure of risk, is slightly more involved. The reason is that a standard deviation is not a linear function of the NPVs (whereas the expected performance is a weighted average of the NPVs, which is a linear function).

To compute the standard deviation for the performance of a portfolio, we must consider all the possible scenarios that affect the entire portfolio. We then compute the performance measure under each scenario and set the probabilities of each scenario. Then, we combine these pieces of information into a standard deviation using the steps in Section 5.2.

To illustrate the computation of a standard deviation for a portfolio let us return to our yoghurt-cum-ice-cream portfolio. Here we must consider nine possible scenarios that consist of pairs such as {best case yoghurt, best case ice cream} and {best case yoghurt, medium case ice cream}. We then compute the NPV under each such scenario by taking 1/3 of the yoghurt expected NPV and 2/3 of the ice cream expected value. For example, under the scenario {best case yoghurt, best case ice cream} the NPV is $1/3 \times 609,453 + 2/3 \times 427,937 = 448,443$ (see Figures 5.3 and 5.4 for the best-case expected NPV numbers for each of the projects). Using this logic, we obtain the NPVs in Table 7.1.

| | | Yoghurt | | |
		Best case	Medium case	Worst case
Ice	Best case	488,443	357,941	240,828
Cream	Medium case	332,710	202,209	85,096
	Worst case	192,672	62,170	-54,942

Table 7.1: NPV for each of the nine scenarios in the portfolio of yoghurt and ice cream projects

Recall that the standard deviation measures how much performance can vary across scenarios. We therefore use the table of NPVs to measure the variability of NPV values around the expected NPV. In particular, we compute the squared deviations of each of the nine NPV numbers from the portfolio's expected NPV (239,557). This allows us to complete steps 1 and 2 described in Section 5.2.

Next, we must assign a probability to each of the nine scenarios. Consider the probabilities given in Table 7.2: Note

| | | Yoghurt | | |
		Best case	Medium case	Worst case
Ice	Best case	0.20	0.08	0.12
Cream	Medium case	0.15	0.07	0.08
	Worst case	0.05	0.15	0.10

Table 7.2: Probabilities for each of the nine scenarios in the portfolio of yoghurt and ice cream projects

that the sum of the probabilities in each row and in each column corresponds to the scenario probability that we used for the individual projects in Section 5.1, namely, Prob(Best case)=0.4, Prob(Worst case)=0.3, and Prob(Medium case)=0.3.

The portfolio's NPV standard deviation is then computed by multiplying each of the squared deviations by its corresponding probability, summing all of these numbers, and finally taking a square root:

$$\text{Standard Dev} = \sqrt{(488,443 - 239,557)^2 \times 0.2 + \cdots + (-54,942 - 239,557)^2 \times 0.1}$$
$$= \text{Nu } 174,129$$

7.4 Comparing a portfolio with individual projects

To compare the portfolio to the individual projects in terms of
anticipated performance and risk, we can use the measures of
expected performance and risk for the portfolio as well as for the
individual projects. In general, and as noted earlier, the expected
performance of the portfolio is always somewhere between the
expected performance of each of the individual projects. The
surprising result is for the standard deviation: *the risk of a portfolio can be lower than any of the individual projects!* The result that
a portfolio can reduce risk is well known in the financial world,
and is one of the principles of financial investments.

This is also the case in our example, as can be seen in Table 7.3. Figure 7.2 displays the same numbers graphically. The
location of each project (yoghurt, ice cream, and combined) is
determined by its expected NPV (on the x-axis) and risk (on the
y-axis)[1] . The "good" area in the plot is the *bottom right*: high expected NPV and low risk. We see that the ice cream project is the
worst performer, with lowest expected NPV and medium risk.
Executing the yoghurt project is expected to yield the highest
NPV, but it is also by far the riskiest (high standard deviation).
The combined yoghurt and ice cream project (1/3 on yoghurt
production and 2/3 on ice cream production) has an expected
NPV that falls between the NPV of each individual project, but is
the least risky of all options.

[1] To create this chart in Excel, create a column with expected NPVs and a column with standard deviations. Then use these columns as the two axes in a scatter plot

	Expected NPV (Nu)	Standard Dev (Nu)
Yoghurt	269,149	309,387
Ice cream	224,761	184,768
Combined	239,557	174,129

Table 7.3: Comparing the expected performance and risk of the yoghurt project, the ice-cream project, and the combined yoghurt-cum-ice cream project

Before we de-mystify how the risk of a portfolio can be lower
than any of its individual components, let us examine the effect
of weights of the different projects within the portfolio. In our
example, we looked at producing yoghurt 1/3 of the week and
ice cream 2/3 of the week. How will producing more or less
yoghurt affect the expected NPV and risk? How to choose the
right balance?

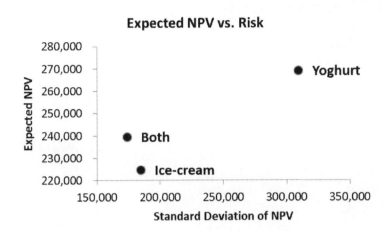

Figure 7.2: Comparing the three projects (yoghurt only, ice cream only, and combined) in terms of expected NPV and risk. Yoghurt has the highest expected NPV; The combined project has the lowest risk

7.5 Effect of weights on portfolio performance

To explore the effect of different combinations of projects in a portfolio, we can use Excel's data tables. To optimize weights, we can also use Solver.

Recall that the weights across the portfolios must add up to 1 (or 100%). Hence, for a portfolio of two projects a one-way data table is sufficient for modifying the weight of one project, which automatically adjusts the weight of the other project. In our portfolio, we combined two projects (yoghurt and ice cream) and therefore a one-way data table is sufficient for exploring the effect of changing the weight of yoghurt. To explore the effect of different weights on the portfolio's expected NPV and standard deviation, we create a one-way data table such as the one shown in Figure 7.3. On the bottom left is the one-way data table setup, based on the computations in the top. We choose the weights of interest for yoghurt in column *A* (weights between 0 and 1 with step size of choice). Our *table outputs* of interest are the formulas for expected NPV and standard deviation in cells B25:C25, which we take from cells B24:C24 (where they are computed). Finally, our *table input* is the weight for yoghurt, which we take from cell B18. This will be entered as the "row input cell" in the data table menu (*Data > What − If Analysis > DataTable*). Note that the

cell for ice cream weight in cell C18 is given by $= 1 - B18$, to
assure that the weights for yoghurt and ice cream add up to 1.
The resulting table is shown in the right side of figure 7.3.

C18		f_x =1-B18	
	A	B	C
16	Combined		
17		yogurt	ice-cream
18	weights	0.33333	0.66667
19			
20	Expected NPV	239,557	
21			
22	standard deviation	174,129	
23			
24		Expected NPV	Standard Dev
25	yogurt weight	239,557	174,129
26	0.0		
27	0.1		
28	0.2		
29	0.3		
30	0.4		
31	0.5		
32	0.6		
33	0.7		
34	0.8		
35	0.9		
36	1.0		

		Expected NPV	Standard Dev
24			
25	yogurt weight	239,557	174,129
26	0.0	BTN 224,761	BTN 184,768
27	0.1	BTN 229,200	BTN 174,463
28	0.2	BTN 233,639	BTN 170,079
29	0.3	BTN 238,077	BTN 172,067
30	0.4	BTN 242,516	BTN 180,219
31	0.5	BTN 246,955	BTN 193,756
32	0.6	BTN 251,394	BTN 211,648
33	0.7	BTN 255,833	BTN 232,894
34	0.8	BTN 260,271	BTN 256,662
35	0.9	BTN 264,710	BTN 282,316
36	1.0	BTN 269,149	BTN 309,387

Figure 7.3: Comparing the
three projects (yoghurt only,
ice cream only, and com-
bined) in terms of expected
NPV and risk. Yoghurt has
the highest expected NPV;
The combined project has
the lowest risk

Charts are much better than tables for displaying trends and
patterns. We therefore create two charts, similar to those created earlier for comparing performance, for exploring the effect
of weights on expected performance and risk. The first chart
(Figure 7.4) shows the linear increase in expected NPV as we
produce more yoghurt and less ice cream, as we've already seen
in Figure 7.1. The new and interesting part is the line denoting standard deviation, which shows that the risk is minimized
when we produce around 20% yoghurt (and 80% ice cream).
From the one-way data table (Figure 7.3) we can verify that the
lowest standard deviation is achieved at the "yoghurt weight" of
0.2.

We can also look at the one-way data table numbers from a
different angle, by plotting the relationship between expected
NPV and risk as we vary the weights of yoghurt. Figure 7.5
displays a curve where the proportion of yoghurt production
increases from 0 to 1 (as noted by the labels on the curve). We
see that the expected performance increases as the proportion
increases, but that risk first decreases before starting to increase.

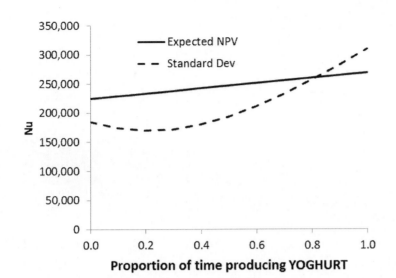

Figure 7.4: The effect of different weights of yoghurt production (and ice cream production) on the performance of their combination. Risk is minimized at a "yoghurt weight" of 0.2

This chart is useful for choosing weights given some requirements on risk or on expected performance. For example, if the Ministry of Agriculture requires only an expected NPV of Nu 220,000 for the project to be considered viable, but wants to minimize risk as much as possible (given that the main objectives of the project are not financial), the best portfolio would be to produce (approximately) yoghurt 20% of the time yoghurt and ice cream 80% of the time. Alternatively, if the requirement is to limit the risk to a standard deviation of Nu 200,000, then the best portfolio is producing yoghurt and ice cream (approximately) in equal amounts of time.

Excel can be used to find the weights that optimize expected performance or risk under some constraints, using Solver. Recall that we must determine three components:

1. The Objective (Target) - what are we trying to optimize?

2. Variable Cells - which factors will be modified to optimize the objective?

3. Constraints - what are requirements and limitations on various measurements?

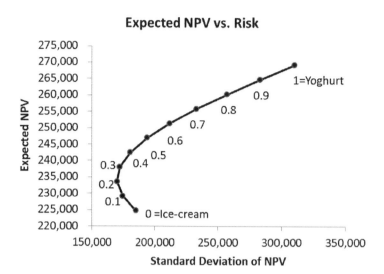

Figure 7.5: The effect of different weights of yoghurt production (and ice cream production) on the performance of their combination. Weights, denoting the proportion of yoghurt production, are marked on the line. Extremes are "only yoghurt" and "only ice cream". The ideal location on the chart is the top left, denoting high expected performance and low risk

In our context, the objective might be maximizing expected performance or minimizing risk. The variable cells are the weights of the different projects. The constraints include the requirement that all weights must be non-negative and less than 1 (we also assure that weights add up to 1 by setting one of the weights to be equal to 1 minus the sum of the other weights). Other constraints might include requirements on expected performance or risk.

To illustrate the use of Solver for finding optimal weights in a portfolio, consider the example where the Ministry of Agriculture wants to minimize risk under the requirement that expected NPV must be at least Nu 220,000. Figure 7.6 shows the spreadsheet setup for this task, the completed Solver menu, and the solution. The constraints assure that the weights are between 0-1 and that the expected NPV (cell B20) is at least Nu 220,000. The objective is set as minimizing the standard deviation (cell B22).

Solver's solution gives weights of 0.25 for yoghurt and 0.75 for ice cream. This solution gives an expected NPV of exactly Nu 220,000 with a standard deviation of Nu 158,719. It is good

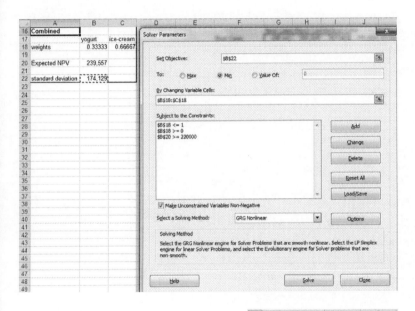

Figure 7.6: Using Solver to find the optimal weights of projects in a portfolio. Top: setting up the spreadsheet and entering parameters into Solver's menu. Bottom: Solver's solution

practice to go back to the charts to confirm that the solution is logical. The chart also gives us a better understanding of how this solution differs from other choices of weights. For instance, we can see in Figure 7.5 that the risk curve in the area of the yoghurt weight 0.25 is quite stable, meaning that changing the weight slightly up or down will not lead to a large change in risk. Since we are considering a 6-workday week, producing yoghurt 1/4 of the time means switching the type of production in the middle of a day. This might not be practical, and therefore we'd opt for weights that are in full days. The nearest weights are 1/6 (=0.167) and 2/6 (=0.333). Comparing the performance of these options on the charts immediately shows us that 1/6 does not achieve the minimum expected NPV, and therefore we resort to 2/6, which happens to coincide with the portfolio that we discussed extensively throughout this chapter.

7.6   When portfolios shine: Choosing the right projects

We are now ready to de-mystify the risk-reducing potential of diversification, which will clarify what projects are best combined into a portfolio.

When will investing in a combination of projects be less risky than investing in a single project? It depends on the relation between the outcomes of the different projects. Let us consider three cases:

Positively correlated projects - the outcomes of the different projects are linked so that all projects are likely to succeed or fail together

Uncorrelated projects - the outcomes of the different projects are independent of each other

Negatively correlated projects - the outcomes of the different projects are linked so that when some projects succeed, others fail and vice versa

Under which of the three cases is a portfolio most useful for reducing risk? If the different projects' success chances are positively correlated, then investing in a single project or in a group of projects will likely have the same risk level. Hence, combining projects with outcomes that are likely to co-succeed and co-fail will not reduce risk. For example, the yoghurt and ice cream projects are likely to be positively correlated, because they rely on the same raw materials and resources. A shortage of local milk, manpower issues, transportation blockages, and financial downturns are likely to affect both projects in the same direction. The same would be the case if we combined projects that produce yoghurt of different flavors.

A related distinction is between *substitute goods* and *complementary goods*. In economics, substitute goods are those where increasing the price of one good leads to increased demand of the other good. For example, increases in the price of UHT milk might lead to more demand for fresh milk. Increasing the price of pre-paid mobile plans might increase demand for post-paid plans. Substitute products therefore contribute to negative correlation between projects. In contrast, complementary goods are those where decreasing the price of one good increase the demand for the other good. For example, lowering the price of mobile phones will likely increase purchases of mobile plans. Hence, substitute goods contribute to positive correlation between projects. To figure out whether goods (or services) are likely to be complementary or substitute we ask questions such as: Do customers purchase both product simultaneously? If one type is purchased, will the other most likely not be purchased?

When the outcomes of the different projects are independent of each other (uncorrelated projects), combining the projects into a portfolio will reduce risk compared to the individual projects, but there is always a chance that several projects might fail together. An example of such a combination is sales of milk and eggs (and a growing number of shops in Thimphu specialize in this combination). Organizations that rely on telecommunication, such as call centers, can reduce risk by investing in independent internet access technologies such as DSL and mobile broadband. An example is a new project recently launched by a private-public venture between the Ministry of Agriculture in Bhutan and a group of entrepreneurs from the United States[2]) for growing hazelnuts in Eastern Bhutan. While most agriculture

[2] See Ministry of Agriculture's announcement at www.moa.gov.bt/moa/news/news_detail.php?id=570

in Bhutan is targeted at self-sustenance, the government has been encouraging farmers to grow cash crops to increase their income, to help curb urban migration, and as a diversification of the country's income. The hazelnut project and the yoghurt project, which are both currently underway and under the Ministry of Agriculture, are uncorrelated.

This leaves us with the third case of negative correlation: if the outcomes of the projects in a portfolio are likely to take opposite directions, this is the best way to reduce risk! It guarantees that when one project fails, the other(s) will likely succeed. Combinations of this type are used to tackle the challenge of seasonality. In North America, for instance, individuals who offer snow-removal services in winter also offer lawn-mowing services in summer. Combining projects that rely on different energy sources, such as oil and gas, can reduce risk (financial investment in this combination is known to reduce risk because of the negative correlation between prices of oil and gas). Similarly, projects that produce substitute products (such as milk with various levels of fat content; areas with low-end and high-end hotels; tour companies with difficult and easy treks) will contribute to negative correlation.

To illustrate the effect of negative correlation on risk reduction, let us return to the yoghurt-cum-ice cream project portfolio. To convey a strong negative correlation between the projects, we modify the nice scenario probabilities from Table 7.2 such that the success of one project is likely to occur with a failure of the other. Table 7.4 shows such an example. Here, the probability of "best case" yoghurt and "worst case" ice cream is high, while the probability "best case" yoghurt and "best case" ice cream is low, and similarly "worst case" yoghurt and "worst case" ice cream is low (in fact, we make the last two probabilities equal to zero). Note that although the nine probabilities are modified, the sums of the probabilities in each row and in each column continue to correspond to the scenario probability that we used for the individual projects in Section 5.1, namely, Prob(Best case)=0.4, Prob(Worst case)=0.3, and Prob(Medium case)=0.3.

Figures 7.7-7.8 are reproductions of Figures 7.4-7.5 with the new scenario probabilities. The grey lines denote the previous

		Yoghurt		
		Best case	Medium case	Worst case
Ice	Best case	0	0.15	0.25
Cream	Medium case	0.10	0.15	0.05
	Worst case	0.30	0	0

Table 7.4: Probabilities for each of the nine scenarios in the portfolio of yoghurt and ice cream projects, yielding negative correlation

performance, for easy comparison. We see that negative correlation does not affect the expected performance at all, but it does reduce risk considerably. Note also that the lowest risk is now achieved at a higher weight of 0.4 (compared to 0.2 previously), indicating that in this new scenario we should produce yoghurt approximately 40% of the time and ice cream 60% of the time. In other words, the choice of portfolio weights should also depend on the correlation between projects.

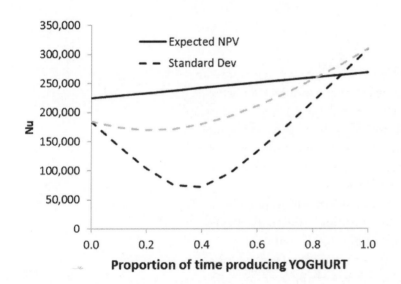

Figure 7.7: Negatively correlated projects and reduced risk: Expected performance (black line) and risk (black broken line) at different choices of weights (proportion of yoghurt production). The broken grey line denotes the risk curve from Figure 7.4, showing that the risk is lowered with negatively correlated projects

There are two important implications of the effect of correlation between projects and risk reduction. First, from the point of view of risk, *good portfolios include projects that are ideally negatively correlated, or at least uncorrelated.* Examples include renewable energy projects such as hydropower, solar energy, and wind power; cultivation of different varieties of rice; use of farmland for crops,

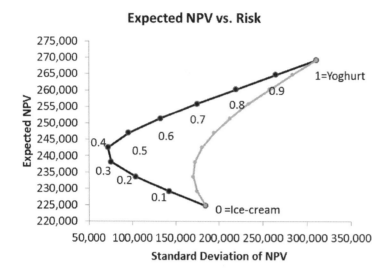

Figure 7.8: Negatively correlated projects and reduced risk: Expected performance and risk as a function of different weights of yoghurt production (weights marked on line). Black line corresponds to negatively-correlated projects. Grey line corresponds to Figure 7.5. The ideal location on the chart is the top left, denoting high expected performance and low risk

livestock, and energy generation. Note that such portfolios are useful for reducing risk. However, when considering portfolios over specialization, the investor's context must be taken into account. For example, while at the individual farm level it might make more sense to specialize, at the national level a portfolio of farms can be advantageous to the agricultural sector. Similarly, diversification in fields of study in higher education makes more sense at the national level than at the individual student's level (although some diversification within an individual's degree lowers the risk of choosing an inappropriate path!).

The second implication of the effect of correlation on risk reduction relates to the number of projects in a portfolio. The term *correlation* implies a relationship between a pair of projects. The more projects in a portfolio, the more pairs to consider, and the lesser the chance of all those pairs exhibiting negative or no correlation. Hence, it is important to *limit the number of projects in a portfolio.*

To conclude, project portfolios are a strategy for reducing the risk involved in project investment. While we discussed risk mainly in monetary terms, the principles of investment, risk and risk reduction apply to all resources – time, pain, effort, etc. If logistically feasible, it is often worth the extra effort to execute a combination of projects rather than a single one.

Exercises

Bhutan Dairy And Agro Products is a private limited company in Bhutan. It specializes in tetra-packed drinks including one-litre single-toned milk and double-toned milk under the brand "Duyul", and 200 ml mango juice. The March 12, 2011 article in the Kuensel newspaper describes some operational details and challenges that the company faces. Read the article[3] and answer the following questions:

[3] The article is available in Figure 7.10 or online at kuenselonline.com/2010/modules.php?name=News&file=article&sid=18681 (last accessed Sept 1, 2011)

1. Consider the three products on offer (single-toned milk, double-toned milk, and mango juice). Which factors affect production of all three in the same direction? Which factors affect production of the three products differently?

2. Which factors affect sales of all three products in the same direction? Which factors affect sales of the three products differently? Are sales of the three products likely to be correlated positively, negatively, or uncorrelated? Remember that a correlation must be between two projects.

3. The company plans to re-launch two tetra-packed drinks: apple and litchi juice as well as bottled water. How do these products relate to the existing three products? Consider factors common to all five products as well as factors that affect them differently.

4. The company is considering expanding to markets in Northeast India. Under what conditions will such diversification reduce financial risk?

Figure 7.9: Image from Kuensel newspaper's March 12, 2011 article

Saturday
March 12, 2011
KUENSEL

BUSINESS ✳ 13

Bhutan Dairy And Agro Products

Now a private (limited) company

KINGA DEMA, P/LING

The Bhutan dairy and agro products ltd (BDAPL) in Phuentsholing, the first company to be de-listed from the royal securities exchange, is now in business as a private ltd. company.

▌DAIRY & AGRO

The company was de-listed last year, as it failed to declare dividends even once since it got listed in 1994.

It has rechristened itself as Bhutan Milk and Agro private ltd, although it is producing the same products as earlier under two promoters - former promoter, Ugyen Wangdi, and the new promoter, Sacha Rinchen Dorji, who also took over as the managing director.

The total worth of the company, after the new management and promoters, now stands at about Nu 200M as per the present market valuations. As the company suffered a huge loss, shareholders were paid a 15 percent premium and their shares bought by Ugyen Wangdi and Shacha Rinchen Dorji.

Operations began in August last year and production from November. "Since then, production has been consistent," Sacha Rinchen Dorji said. Its products in the market as of now are the one-litre toned milk and double toned milk under the brand, Duyul, and the 200ml mango juice in tetra packs.

At present, it operates at about 25 to 30 percent of the total production capacity owing to space constraints, according to the management. The optimum plant capacity is about 80,000litres of milk in a day, and 24,000litres of juice in 20 hours.

Getting back to business wasn't easy, Sacha Rinchen Dorji said. Liabilities with the government had to be updated first. "For 60 percent operations or productions, the required budget was about Nu 70M," he said.

With the company shut down for several months, the sophisticated computerised machines had broken down, on which about Nu 6M was spent on repairs. The company, also managed to negotiate and reschedule its loan with the Swedish firm from where they had bought a Nu 100M state of the art ultra high temperature (UHT) tetrapacking machine in 2006.

"The firm waived off the outstanding interests and penalties," he said. "It was also negotiated that the loan repayment will be made through instalments within seven years, starting this September."

Lack of space being a major constraint, additional infrastructure, such as warehouse to store raw materials and finished products and additional water reservoirs are being built that are expected to be completed by April end.

The management also claims to have recruited competent employees. Employees, who weren't paid for about seven months, were given their salaries and double increment; while the key persons were given double promotion as well. At present, there are about 50 employees.

The management said that apple and litchi juice in tetra packs will be relaunched by July, while the company will also be launching its packaged drinking water in May. "We're also exploring market beyond Bhutan," said Shacha Rinchen Dorji. "The management's in negotiation with prospective dealers and distributors in northeast India."

Started as a government enterprise, it was privatised in 1994, with a paid up capital of Nu 2.5M invested by 96 shareholders.

In 1994, it took off on a good footing, producing about 5,000 litres of pasturised milk everyday in plastic packets. But it soon ran into problems, when milk supply from cooperatives began to dry up and production slid by almost 10 times. In 2001, it showed signs of recovery making an earning of Nu 830,000, and its share price climbing back to its face value of Nu 100 a share from a low of Nu 40 a share. That year, the agriculture ministry and BDFCL also waived off a total debt of Nu 4.1M to help its revival.

The company had an accumulated loss of Nu 48.34M in 2006, which increased to Nu 75.36M in 2007. Its loans were Nu 138.7M and total assets were Nu 152.16M in 2007.

Figure 7.10: Article about Bhutan Dairy and Agro Products in Kuensel newspaper. Available at kuenselonline.com/ 2010/modules.php?name= News&file=article&sid= 18681

Index

2752549R00061

Printed in Great Britain
by Amazon.co.uk, Ltd.,
Marston Gate.